1,000,000 Books

are available to read at

Forgotten Books

www.ForgottenBooks.com

Read online
Download PDF
Purchase in print

ISBN 978-0-260-07926-8
PIBN 11021922

This book is a reproduction of an important historical work. Forgotten Books uses state-of-the-art technology to digitally reconstruct the work, preserving the original format whilst repairing imperfections present in the aged copy. In rare cases, an imperfection in the original, such as a blemish or missing page, may be replicated in our edition. We do, however, repair the vast majority of imperfections successfully; any imperfections that remain are intentionally left to preserve the state of such historical works.

Forgotten Books is a registered trademark of FB &c Ltd.
Copyright © 2018 FB &c Ltd.
FB &c Ltd, Dalton House, 60 Windsor Avenue, London, SW19 2RR.
Company number 08720141. Registered in England and Wales.

For support please visit www.forgottenbooks.com

1 MONTH OF FREE READING

at

www.ForgottenBooks.com

By purchasing this book you are eligible for one month membership to ForgottenBooks.com, giving you unlimited access to our entire collection of over 1,000,000 titles via our web site and mobile apps.

To claim your free month visit: www.forgottenbooks.com/free1021922

* Offer is valid for 45 days from date of purchase. Terms and conditions apply.

English
Français
Deutsche
Italiano
Español
Português

www.forgottenbooks.com

Mythology Photography **Fiction**
Fishing Christianity **Art** Cooking
Essays Buddhism Freemasonry
Medicine **Biology** Music **Ancient Egypt** Evolution Carpentry Physics
Dance Geology **Mathematics** Fitness
Shakespeare **Folklore** Yoga Marketing
Confidence Immortality Biographies
Poetry **Psychology** Witchcraft
Electronics Chemistry History **Law**
Accounting **Philosophy** Anthropology
Alchemy Drama Quantum Mechanics
Atheism Sexual Health **Ancient History**
Entrepreneurship Languages Sport
Paleontology Needlework Islam
Metaphysics Investment Archaeology
Parenting Statistics Criminology
Motivational

EXPERIENCE

OF THE LATE

MRS. FRANCES PAWSON,

WIDOW OF THE LATE REV. JOHN PAWSON,

WHO WAS ABOUT FORTY-FOUR YEARS AN ITINERANT PREACHER IN THE METHODIST CONNEXION:

BY

JOSEPH SUTCLIFFE.

WITH A PREFACE, BY JOSEPH ENTWISLE.

LONDON:

Printed at the Conference-Office, 14, City-Road,
By THOMAS CORDEUX, Agent:

Sold by T. Blanshard, 14, City-Road; also at all the Methodist Preaching-Houses in Town and Country.

1813.

P358

PREFACE.

AT the request of my friend, Mr. Sutcliffe, I carefully examined and revised the following noir, drawn up by him, pursuant to a promise e to Mrs. Pawson some time before her decease. had an opportunity of observing her spirit, temper, manner of life during his residence near her at ls, and close intimacy with her.

he following pages present to the reader a faithportrait of a pious woman. I had the happiness er acquaintance and uninterrupted friendship for ity years; and having lived in the same house her two years, knew her well. *It may be affirmed, we are in reality, what we are in secret befor , and in the bosom of our own family!*

lrs. P. was a person of unaffected humility and stian simplicity. She walked with God, and had conversation in heaven. Few christians spent so h time as she in prayer, and her secret prayers fervent and importunate. She poured out her to God, not for herself and most intimate connex*only*, but also for the church universal, and the ld. Her concern fot the peace and prosperity of community to which she belonged, was deep and

(iv)

found to impede her spiritual progress; and her repeated efforts to rise above them. These things, faithfully recorded in her Journal, are but the repetition of what her christian friends often heard from her own mouth. While reading the account of her various exercises and enjoyments contained in the following narrative, who that knew her can forbear to say, " Though dead, she yet speaketh?"

The serious reader, attending to the subject of the memoir in the successive stages of her pilgrimage, will see her in a great variety of circumstances; will mark the gradual openings of her mind; her progress in the divine life; her lively religious feelings, conflicts, and comforts; her conscientious regard to what she thought the path of duty—and though he may, perhaps, think she was in some particulars too rigid and scrupulous, yet he will perceive, that, "in all her ways, she acknowledged the Lord, and that he directed her paths." Her path was as the shining light, which shineth more and more unto the perfect day."

May all who read her history, imitate her spirit, and be favoured with an exit peaceful as her's.——Amen.

Bristol, JOSEPH ENTWISLE,
May 6, 1813.

OF

MRS. PAWSON.

THE first Christian societies, both in Asia and in Europe, were distinguished by pious and holy women. The Evangelists, and St. Paul, have repeatedly acknowledged their obligations to them in planting churches, and in the social care of the flock. The like instances might, perhaps, be traced in every reformation and revival of religion since that period. Providence has assigned them a sphere of usefulness, and especially to their own sex, which men were less qualified to perform. They were deaconnesses, catechists, or class-leaders, if one use a modern name, to their own sex. They had an access to the female branches of families, disallowed to men by the manners of the East.

The history of Methodism is not less distinguished than the other revivals of religion by women of extraordinary piety and zeal, who have stood forth for the help of the Lord of hosts. Almost every large society in the Methodist connection can boast of women, whose faith, nourished by a lively expectation of the coming and kingdom of our Lord Jesus Christ, has prompted them to make every sacrifice to which they were called, and to devote their time, their talents, and their fortunes, wholly to his glory. They have trampled on the vanities of conformity to the world, and regulated the whole of their life on the noble principle, to be approved and owned of God. The world, indeed, for a while, accounted them fools, and augured their ruin; but "wisdom is justified of her children." They lived in communion with God, in society with the best of people, and, after a life of holiness and usefulness, they died in the assurance of a glorious immortality. Died! did I say? but they live; they live in the recollection and hearts of their friends; and they seem to talk with us daily in the writings on experimental religion which their friends have published. Thus, like the setting sun, they have left their lustre behind, and irradiated the church with the softer graces of every Christian temper.

Their piety had also a peculiar excellence in regard to its effects in social life. It was not confined to a convent, nor narrowed and degraded by the gloom of solitude. The women of education, that espoused the cause of early Methodism, employed their leisure hours in mental improvement, in religious correspondence, in visiting the sick, in the instruction of orphan children, in aiding institutions of benevolence; and while their once gay companions were amusing themselves with parties, or crowding the theatre, these women were found in the house of God, or spending an hour in meetings for social prayer, and religious fellowship.

In regard to benevolence, and the offices of charity, Methodism has realized all that FRONTO has said of women in the primitive church, "that ladies, in whose veins the noblest blood did run, disdained not to visit the sick and afflicted: and doing this in select parties, one of them would sit and talk with the sick, a second would dress her sores, and a third would prepare her something to eat: and she who was thus attended, thought she saw the image of the Lord Jesus in the condescension and kindness of her friends; and they who assisted her, thought they saw the image of Christ in the faith, the patience, the gratitude, and love, of their afflicted sister. Thus they saw the image of God in one another: grace made them all one, of the household of faith, and of the family of heaven."

Nor ought it to escape remark, that their piety did not lose its reward. The world asserted, that conversions so extraordinary, and a conduct so singular, would terminate in poverty and ruin. The contrary, however, has been the consequence. Whatever reverses may have happened to individuals through error, want of counsel, or precipitancy of conduct, Methodism has enriched, and not impoverished, its converts. Many of those young persons of whom I write, after glorifying God in a humble sphere, and becoming distinguished by religion and virtue, have been placed in families far above the expectations of their friends; and means have been afforded of doing all the good for which they sighed while filling a humbler station in life. "Verily, then, there is a reward for the righteous;" yea, not unfrequently, a hundred-fold reward in this world, and in the world to come life everlasting.

FRANCES PAWSON, whose volumnious memoirs are extracted here, was daughter of Mr. Timothy Mortimer, of the city of York. She was born the 11th of May, 1736, and lost her father at the age of fifteen, in the sixty-third year of his age. He left a widow and two sons, the eldest of whom was the Rev. Dr. Charles Mortimer, who preferred a college life, and was chosen rector of Lincoln college, Oxford, a little before his death. The younger brother, Timothy, became a respectable and opulent attorney in York.

Her parents gave her an education suitable to her expectations in life. Few women surpassed her in the neatness and elegance of her handwriting; and many parts of her early journals are correctly written in French. She wrote a good letter, but neglected to form a regular style, which is a great defect in education.

Miss Mortimer was born with more ingenuousness than is common to the human kind

gion, and a strict attendance on devotion in early life, laid the foundation of that amiable Christian she

world, in what is called *innocent amusement*. Till about the age of thirty, she spent her time in dress, in reading novels, in receiving and returning visits. The indiscretions of life may be seen and lamented; but the years so misapplied can never be reclaimed.

In the year 1770, Miss Mortimer had an intimate friend married to a Mr. Nidsdale of London. A visit to town was a consequence of the wedding. This gentleman had an excellence and frankness of character; and, animated by the holy zeal of a young convert, he apprised Miss Mortimer of the rules of his house respecting family devotion, and that none of his guests must attend balls and theatres. His ingenuous manner, and unaffected piety, gained her esteem. By his holy conversation, and by the sermons she heard, her eyes became gradually enlightened to discover the reality of religion; and a conviction was fixed in her breast, that a good man is happy.

Miss Mortimer, early in 1771, returned to York full of good resolutions, and endeavoured to conform all her tempers to the precepts of the Gospel. She was not, however, sufficiently awakened to see the insufficiency of human efforts, and distinguish the plain way of salvation by faith. She had to grope her way in the dark, and amidst a painful variety of opinions and parties. As a previous step, she dismissed her novels, books which powerfully beguile the fancy without improving the mind; and which, for the most part, are written by learned seducers, and ruined women. This refined class of writers affect, indeed, to be masters of the human heart, while their own breast is polluted with the reveries of every vile affection. Instead of reading these books, oftener caricatures than copies of human nature, she commenced a regular course of biblical reading, connected with the perusal of such other religious books as circumstances threw in her way. She went so far also as to read a prayer every morning to her servant maid, and every evening to the family.

But a greater difficulty remained: this change in Miss Mortimer's views and life, became a subject of conversation among a large circle of families with whom she had long been accustomed to visit, and her conduct was exposed to scrutiny, and herself to frequent remonstrances. Here she was guided in the ancient road in which the saints have walked, to sacrifice that worldly friendship which is hurtful to the soul; and firmly to shift its ground to the side of good offices, and best wishes for their spiritual good.

Between Miss Mortimer and a Miss Y—n, there had subsisted a friendship of the most intimate kind; and the displeasure of this young lady against the change in her friend, had, it would seem, been expressed with some degree of tartness. On this subject, Miss Mortimer writes as follows:—

" Nov. 9, 1771. After the maturest deliberation, I have resolved to conduct myself toward Miss Y. in the following manner: Never to allow my happiness to be, for one moment, disturbed by any displeasure she may show to me, as her conduct is the result of passion, and not of reason. But, as so long and close an intimacy has subsisted between us, I will do all in my power, consonant to the principles which duty prescribes, to be on friendly terms with her. If she do not answer the letter I wrote to her yesterday, of which the principal inquiry was her *health*, but adding withal, that I did not wish to know any other particulars, until she could treat me in a more obliging manner: yet, if she write a free letter, then I will continue the correspondence: my letters shall be affectionate, but not servile. By this method, I shall afford her an opportunity, not of forming the same intimacy which used to unite us, but of placing it upon a foundation less liable to separation. And I do this from a conviction, while honoured with her friendship, of having done nothing inconsistent with the means that ought to preserve it.

" I know, by experience, the difficulty of erasing from the memory any thing that has for a long time had possession of it. Arguments have effect only while the mind is impelled to dwell on what has occasioned the disgust; and indulgence of them is the means of keeping the object ever before our eyes, and of recalling the happiness we once enjoyed.

" Nov. 27. This morning I received a very polite letter from Miss Y. She tells me to make my own terms as to our future correspondence: yet I do not desire to request the same intimacy that once subsisted between us.

" April 27, 1772. I have been thinking that I have a character of levity, from my asking questions not of consequence for me to know; and I see that I have failed in my resolutions against it. I cannot keep to the injunctions I have imposed on myself, without the grace of God. I hope, in future, never to give pleasure to others, at the expense of my own satisfaction. I see I must endeavour to support an uniform and regular behaviour, free from all that levity, too often practised to support conversation, and promote mirth. It prevents that conscious rectitude, that endearing self-applause, which alone can satisfy a tender mind. I will, therefore, lay aside all my acquaintance, so soon as I conveniently can; and, finding so little satisfaction in parties, it will be no very difficult task, except with Mrs. ——, whose friendship has been so long and so intimate, that were I to alter my conduct toward her, it would be imputed to a reserve bordering on ingratitude.

"Feb. 28, 1773. Many parts of my past conduct ought to be reflected on with serious concern. Among other things, the time I have devoted to the fashionable amusement of visiting. What a waste of time have I, in this respect, to answer for to God! And what an abuse have I made of the talents that have been given, not to think how improperly they must be cultivated in the circles of tea-parties, where the topics of conversation are, dress, the news of the day, and idle *chit-chat*. I lament that it is now so late in life, in which I have been made sensible of my error and sin. And I fear I shall find it no small difficulty to extricate myself, on account of the humorous character of my acquaintance. They amount to no less in number than seventy families, with whom I have been in the habit of receiving and returning visits.

"To accomplish this reformation, I have thought of various methods, and fixed on the following, which, if it do not prove successful, I hope I shall be directed to something more effectual. *First*, I will not allow myself to visit, or to receive company, except three days in the week, unless a friend shall call without ceremony, and in a way that requires neither dress nor formality. Staying at home is more advisable and edifying, unless I can spend an evening with a friend, whose understanding is cultivated and improved. *Secondly*, Out of fifty families of my acquaintance, there is no need that I should visit, or call upon them, oftener than once a year; and ten of them I may, in a little time, decline altogether. The others I propose never to importune to visit me, but leave it wholly to their choice. My other acquaintance I cannot treat in this manner. They are my neighbours, or friends,

ur to avoid forming any intimacy
vhose principles, understanding, or
art, does not promise to conduce to
or to whom it may not be in my
ful.

Having read to-day the epistle of
ilippians, I felt a desire to write to
and acquaint him with my religious
ooses; not doubting that God had
ent prayers he had offered to heaven
on.

This evening, I spent a most agree-
a select party of Christian friends.
Richardson, (a clergyman of Cum-
ad lately come to York,) expounded
. Mrs. Carr desired him to read
r of Isaiah: he seemed much struck
ises which are there made to the
is the less is always included in the
emed to have a peculiar reference
nent of this little Society in York.
spoke of the comfort which, for
e promises had afforded to her soul.
oke her experience. It was simply
f faith. She related the work of
e beginning, till the time of her

prised that my brother Mortimer was on his way from Oxford to visit us, the news did not disturb the composure of my mind. Hence the interview this morning was easier than I expected.

"August 23. Since my brother's arrival, I have had great depression of mind. Some days I have hardly a moment's rest, groaning under the bondage of sin, and sometimes afflicted at the frowns of the world. Sometimes my mother has reproached me for dropping almost the whole of our acquaintance. To-day my brother M. occasioned me a sore trial, by speaking pointedly to my mother on the necessity of recreations; and that more people were confined in the asylum through religious melancholy, than through any other cause. The Rev. Mr. W. passing the window, I observed, that he looked gay enough. My brother contended, that, from my gravity, I should in two or three years become a maniac. After he was gone, I retired to my chamber, and entreated the Almighty, that no arguments of my brother might affect my constancy, and that I might, when called upon, be enabled to assign a reason of the hope that is in me.

"August 25. My brother M. introduced the subject of religion to me. He avowed his belief in the atonement, and of good works arising from faith. But the knowledge of these doctrines, if we may judge by his conduct, are only in his head. He has no conception of the knowledge of pardon and acceptance with God. The doctrine of Christian perfection he regards as highly absurd, because St. Peter denied his Master, and St. Paul allowed that sin reigned in him. He would not condemn those preachers who inculcated a dry morality; for though they never mentioned our Saviour's name, yet all the virtues they recommended must arise from him. And as to recreations, he highly approved of them, because St. Paul often alludes to the Olympic games of wrestling, fighting, running,

B

which he would not have done had he disapproved of public diversions."

[These extracts tend to show the ignorance that was in the land, prior to the diffusion of religious knowledge. This minister, this doctor in Israel, was not aware, in the first instance, that St. Paul is speaking of the reign of sin in the carnal man, and afterwards of the reign of grace in the spiritual man. And in the second, the allusion to the games is for exertion in the spiritual, and not in the carnal combat. In twenty places, he enjoins the Christians to come out from among the heathen; and adds, that " they think it strange that you run not with them to the same excess of riot."]

" From this time, my brother became more and more imbittered against the Methodists, till at last I told him plainly, that if I were separated from them, there would remain no more enjoyment for me in this world. And my old friends having treated me unkindly, I had now none but religious friends; and I appealed to my mother, and to all the house, if they could say that religion had led me into any impropriety of conduct.

" Sept. 6. On reading Mr. Law's Serious Call to a devout and holy Life, I was very much struck with the force and novelty of his arguments. They seemed to proceed from the Spirit of God. That part where Miranda is mentioned, as never employing herself in work that contributes to vanity, was strikingly applicable to me. A Christian woman, employing herself in the embroidery of dress, has the appearance of one who wishes to please the fashionable world rather than Jesus Christ. Hence I entreated the Lord to enable me to sacrifice every part of my dress, which might in anywise contribute to flatter my vanity.

" Sept. 8. My mother spent the evening at my brother Timothy's. He rallied her and her daughter the whole time concerning religion, and desired my brother Mortimer to talk to me. Brother M. replied, that I was too far gone for any advice of his to be of use. He looked more grave than usual, and did not join in the raillery against religion.

"Sept. 20. We had a party to dine; the conversation turned, between my brother and Mr. R. on history. My brother was far superior to Mr. R. in the mildness of his temper, and in not discovering, as the other did, that he was a bigot to any party. Next morning, my brother and I had a full and free conversation on religion. I was enabled to remove his prejudices against Mr. R. and to place his character and dispositions in a proper light. He approved of my narrowing the circle of my acquaintance, and he expressed no disapprobation of any part of my conduct, though I told him of my attending the weekly meeting at Mrs. Carr's. How great was the goodness of God to me, in softening my brother's heart in my favour! Yet I could not prevail upon him to accompany me to hear Mr. R.

"Oct. 3. This morning I received the Sacrament; but all the afternoon and evening, felt my mind dejected and low. I was dissatisfied with myself, and with every thing about me. Every passion seemed awake. The love of dress returned, and I felt disgusted with the plainness of my adorning. I felt also the remains of many other evil inclinations in my heart. Not one passion seemed subdued. These reviews of my state caused me to weep bitterly for my sins, and fervently to implore pardon.

"Oct. 4. This afternoon I took tea with Mrs. Hebor; she was almost a martyr to the forms of religion. Mr. R. cautioned her against resting in forms; but she said, that on her fast-days, she could always bear her crosses better than on other days.

"Oct. 5. My spirits mos of the day were low.

however, fervent, and accompanied with s
tears. Earnestly did I entreat the Lord,
me that faith which overcomes the worl
the ideas of having given up the pleasure
world, and found no comfort in religion,
me; but prayer, under all such depression
only resource, and it never fails to bring re

"Oct. 26. I have, for a long time, be
with a peevish, fretful temper; I apparen
no love for any one about me; but I see
inward corruptions, and the want of the
God, are the cause of it: yet grace is able
tify every disposition.

"Oct. 29. This morning was ushered
the most exquisite grief I ever remember
experienced. The necessity of sacrificin
holds of vanity by which Satan had so long
me, occasioned me to feel a sort of hell
breast, which shook my whole frame, and I
me to the dust. I was resolved to give
vanity; and yet the thought of being oblig
it, occasioned me extreme torture. This
lasted about two hours; I prayed most of t
and rose from my knees thanking God
enabled me to do it. I now resolved to
cross, and to be, in future, negligent of dre

"Nov. 8. My new resolutions concernii
were no sooner made than tried. Lady A
and Mr. H.'s family, visited us to-day.
course of the conversation, I mentioned \
change in my manner of dressing had

portunity of opening all her heart to Mrs. Carr, a lady of sincere and unaffected piety, but a Mystic in principle. She acquainted her with all the distaste and frequent reluctance she felt to devotion; and with her discouragement at still finding herself in the irritable and dejected state of which she had so frequently complained. These sensations were partly owing to the weakness of her nerves. But Mrs. Carr, consonant to her favourite authors, recommended her to be perfectly resigned to the will of God; and if he saw it good to bring her out of that state, he would do it! Had Mrs. Carr's advice respected providential deliverance, it would have been highly proper: " It is good that a man should both hope, and quietly wait for the salvation of God," Lam. iii. 26. But in spiritual troubles, we should always expect a present blessing. So is the general language of the Psalms; and they are admirable copies of the human heart. So is the language of the New Testament: " The word is nigh thee, even in thy heart and mouth. Believe on the Lord Jesus Christ, and thou shalt be saved." The penitent, like the beggar, is importunate: after making his supplication for a sense of God's pardoning love, he would still add,

" And if thou canst so greatly bow,
Friend of sinners, why not now?"

What is that Mysticism against which Bossuet, Ostervald, Saurin, and so many divines, exclaim? I answer, with deference to those who are much better acquainted with the subject than I am, It is genuine piety, disfigured by the jargon of the schoolmen, and the gloom of the convent. It is that secret flame of piety which kindled in the dark ages of the church, and was promoted by reading spiritual books. Thomas Aquinas, a schoolman, invented many of their terms. Thomas à Kempis, in his " Imitation of Jesus Christ," presented the world with an admirable specimen of their piety. The

Why then is Mysticism to be blamed
what does it differ from primitive Chr
Mysticism is much to be admired for mal
the sole happiness of the soul, and indej
of every creature.

"Dieu, Dieu, Dieu, Je ne veux que
C'est le seul bien que J'aime."
                                St. Fran. d'

But Mysticism is highly to be conde
extravagance in preferring hell to paradis
ded it were the will of God. Hear t
words: "Le bon plaisir de Dieu est le
object de l'âme indifférente, en sorte qu'e
roit mieux l'enfer avec la volonté de Die
paradis sans la volonté de Dieu. Elle
même l'enfer au paradis, si elle savoit q
un peu plus du bon plaisir de Dieu." *I*
Meaux Instruct. p. 331.

Hence, when Miss Mortimer went in 1
Mrs. Carr, she gave advice in the very
the directors and spiritual guides of the
communion, viz. "to be still and quiet, a
God saw it meet to bring her out of tha
would do it!" This is directing the seek
vation to aspire at perfection before he is
it is, in some sort, over-looking justificatic

greatly embarrasses the seeker, and protracts conversion, by not prescribing the immediate and evangelical remedy for the weary and heavy laden.

Hence the religious world, under God, are infinitely in debt to the venerable Wesley for explaining the way of salvation with the utmost propriety of doctrine, and felicity of expression. For many years he sought justification partly by his own works, and partly by Jesus Christ. For three years he conversed at large with Moravian ministers, and was well read in mystical books. And it is apparent, from his christian library of fifty volumes, that no man was better acquainted with the writings of the English Puritans. But, being called to study conversions in a most extensive revival of religion, God enabled him to lay down the scriptural way of salvation by faith in Jesus Christ. He cried to the awakened and contrite sinners, " Behold the Lamb of God, that taketh away the sin of the world." He directed them to come guilty for a pardon, and miserable for mercy, that the spirit of bondage might be superseded by the spirit of adoption, and by the knowledge of salvation through the remission of sins. He directed penitents and believers, in all their various states, to expect instantaneous blessings, consonant to the examples in the holy Scriptures, and to the doctrine of Macarius in his homilies. On finding this scriptural way of salvation, he gave up all mystics; and he equally relieved the doctrine of justification from the confusion which Zuinglius had thrown upon it by the imputation of a double righteousness, *viz.* a passive righteousness to remove our guilt, and an active righteousness to justify our persons, which implies a third, or inherent, righteousness from the Holy Spirit; for the fruit of the Spirit is love, joy, peace, righteousness, &c. I am confident in asserting, that the theology of the Christian church never exhibited a happier code of instructions, for awakened sinners, than is to be

found in the sermons and letters of this hon(
instrument in the Lord's hands.

Nov. 18. Miss Mortimer having continu
long time in a state of dissatisfaction witl
state, and in distressing doubts, called upon
John Spence, and, after opening her mind to
she added, " But I must wait patiently till it
please the Lord to give me acceptance iı
Beloved." He replied, that there was an in
priety in my manner of seeking the blessir
pardon, and that many people would recei
sooner, were they to live in constant expectati
it. He added, that the blessing was a free
and not the reward of any sacrifices we ɪ
make for religion. He then opened the pro
concerning a present salvation, and enlarge
the ability and readiness of Christ to receiv
those that come unto him. He shewed me
Christ was nigh at hand to all them that call
him; and how he has joined the duty anc
promise, ' Ask, and ye shall receive; seek, aɪ
shall find.' I felt thankful afterward that]
called on this good man, for I had been se(
the blessing too much as the reward of my
denial, and of giving up my own will.

" Nov. 19. Mr. Spence took tea with us to
and spoke freely on the way of salvation by f
but, after he was gone, I felt that he had huɪ
pride, by saying, that he thought my mothei
much nearer the blessing than I.

" Nov. 21. Wishful to get help for my so
attended Mr. Spence's class. This is a w
meeting, of about dozen friends, for convers
on Christian experience, and for prayer. W
heard in this meeting, and what the leader
said of my mother being in a better state of
than myself, occasioned me much inquietude.
the evening I prayed and wept bitterly for
two hours, at the throne of grace, for the ble
of pardon and acceptance. My heart seem(

n inexpressible agony. I saw that I had
good thought of my own; and from that
lelivered myself up to the Almighty, more
han ever, to be saved; and if it be the
will that I should, in future, attend the
lists' meeting, he will shew it me: at pre-
o not see my way clear respecting it.

v. 28. Mrs. Carr having called yesterday,
ier all my trial about attending the Metho-
ipel. She advised me to go, if I felt my
lrawn to go. On that account my heart
·ely distressed all the morning, for I had
izing weight on my spirits, lest the Lord
draw me to go in the evening. Satan
iarassed me by injections of pride; and a
f darkness rested on my mind.
t whilst I remained in darkness, my mother
)ught into light. It was but lately that she
braced the idea of feeling her acceptance in
oved. It is impossible to describe the joy that
. Both in reading and in conversation she
to abound in spiritual improvements, and
nazing ease. A new song was put into her
even of praises to our God, Psal. xl. 1, 2, 3.

had sufficient reason to regard this as the d
her acceptance with God.

"Nov. 29. Mrs. Carr, on hearing the
news, seemed much pleased with the manifest
my mother had received, but wished her st
pray for a clearer evidence. At this intervi
told Mrs. Carr the struggles I had felt respe
an occasional attendance on the Methodist pr
ing. She spoke well of the preacher, and sa
I chose to accompany her, I might put on a
cloak and bonnet, and no one would know
The enemy tempted me to levity at the idea o
dress; but this good woman dropped me a g
caution against levity, and advised me to
against giving way to it. Notwithstanding
disposition I was in, 'the great truths delivere
the preacher, made an impression on my mind
they were applicable to my state. The text
"Behold, I stand at the door and knock,'
On returning home my mother seemed no
displeased with me for going to the chapel, v
I took as a proof of the grace she had rece
for her prejudices against Methodism were
strong.

"Nov. 30. To-day I called on Mrs. Carr
talked to her freely on dress, food, &c.
valuable friend, perceiving that I had made
use of FENELON on Pure Love, not intende
the author, and that I had sought a righteou
separate from the atonement, urged a full rel
on the blood of Christ. She assured me,
going dirty would not eradicate the pride o
heart, as no evil passion could be eradicated b
the entrance of Jesus Christ. I perceived,
her conversation, that I had been working in
own strength, and that the Lord did not re
the austerities I had imposed on myself, w
view to subdue my vanity and my pride. But
what a day and night followed! When the e

perceived Babel was about to fall, he assailed me sorely with his empoisoned injections. Because I had begun to indulge myself a little in dress, and had resumed my former diet, he suggested that I had offended God, and that God would now forsake me.

"Dec. 3. To-day I unbosomed my heart afresh to Mrs. Carr. After much conversation on the way in which I was led, she said, it was because the Lord was preparing me to be a mother in Israel, and that she had been for some time of this opinion; hence she regarded all the trials through which I had passed, as designated to answer the wise designs of Providence. Mrs. [Bathsheba] Hall, on the other hand, seeing I had partially resumed my dress, cautioned me to keep between the extremes of self-righteousness and antinomianism. She was very open and communicative.

"Dec. 9. To-day I had a free and open conversation with Miss Sarah Scott, and she seemed to take all I said in good part; indeed, she desired me to remind her whenever I saw any thing amiss in her conduct. There seems to be quite a work of grace begun in her heart.

"Dec. 22. Miss Scott called again, and told me she heard my brother Mortimer say, that if any thing should happen to my mother, he would take me away from York to keep his house. All my pride revived at the ideas of grandeur, pleasure, &c. Ah! this pride, this dormant pride, which has been my sore and besetting sin.

"Jan. 2, 1774. To-day I accompanied Mr. Buckle's family to the Methodist chapel, and felt no cross, as before, either in going, or in coming away. I was much struck with the hymns, and pleased with the sermon. Taking up a volume of Mr. Whitefield's letters, after my return, I was struck also with what he says on our obligation to confess the Saviour before men, in his ministers and his people. But my mother seems displeased

whenever the Methodists' meeting is me[t]
she leaves me, however, to use my pleasu[re]
going; and I believe she is mistaken in the [impres-]
sion lately made on her mind, of confining [me]
wholly to one minister.

"Jan. 8. Walking alone, I had anot[her con-]
flict concerning attending the Methodist [meeting;]
but I perceived that every one of my [objections]
sprung from pride: this carried a convicti[on that]
both my mother and I were held in chains [by the]
head, and that Satan would never take [such]
pains, if it were not to keep us from som[ething.]
Why should he fight against himself?— [Tried]
again; but there was a familiarity in M[r. ——'s]
expressions and manner which dissatisfied [me. I]
returned in doubt whether to attend any m[ore.]

"Jan. 15. I awoke this morning in gr[eat hea-]
viness of spirits; several objections darted [into my]
mind against attending the Methodists' [meeting.]
My mother is displeased about it, and [seems]
more and more against it. I went and [heard a]
good sermon, but did not find much profit.

"Jan. 19. I drank tea to-day at Mr. [——'s]
with Mr. Richardson, and with Mr. (Jose[ph Mil-]
ner, an awakened clergyman, of Hull. [His]
dress is very unfavourable to him; notwi[thstand-]
ing, he appears to be a man of uncommo[n]

and the mere idea of the possibility of this ever happening, threw me into an agony I cannot describe, and it discovered how far my heart was still from God. I related my situation to Mr. ———; and he exhorted me not to encumber my mind with any thing but seeking the Lord: but his remarks on my reading Mr. Whitefield's works, and joining the Methodists, were not of a favourable nature.

"Feb. 10. At Mrs. Carr's meeting, though I heard an excellent discourse, yet my heart was as hard as a stone. Mr. R.'s discourses are exceedingly fine, yet there seems a bar which prevents my being benefited by them in the way that I hope will one day be the case. In regard of edification, it is otherwise when I hear Mr. Helton: never did I sit under a preacher with so much pleasure. Surely, then, it is a temptation of Satan which keeps me from the Methodist meeting. Why should the sheep not graze where they find the sweetest grass?

"Feb. 19. I read a prayer in Alleine's Alarm, and found that he advises sinners to make a covenant with God, to renounce, from that time, through grace, whatever they know to be contrary to his will; to preserve the writing as a memorial of the solemn transaction; and to spread it before the Lord in all times of doubt and temptation. The method struck me as highly proper, and I hastened to do it, without delay, in the following words:—

"O God, I here kneel, and am determined, through thy grace, without which I can do nothing, henceforth to devote my body, and my soul, with all its powers, to thee; and to resist every thing that is contrary to thy will, that thou mayst enable me to say as I once did before the throne of grace, Behold me, Lord, and do with me whatever thou wilt. And now, O Almighty God, thou knowest that I make this covenant with thee this day, with-

C

thee, that, if thou seest any flaw or reserva
it, that thou wouldst discover it, and help
do it aright. And from this 19th day of Fel
1774, I would humbly call thee mine.

"FRANCES MORTI*

"Feb 27. To-day I heard Mr. Hunter p
he magnified the Redeemer's righteousness
sole ground of a sinner's justification, and i
on his holiness being imparted to us; the
said, were to be apprehended by faith.
glad, because I had often heard Mr. R. sa*
the Methodists denied the imputation of (
righteousness: whereas, on inquiry, I foun
they only guarded the doctrine against the
dities to which antinomianism might lead.
James Hervey, or rather his editor of elev
ters, has quite misrepresented Mr. Wesley'
trine, and written under a misguided influen

"March 15. Yesterday, at twelve o'clock
at prayer, my heart of stone gave way:
much, and found great enlargement in wr
for my relatives.

"May 24. This afternoon I attended th*
feast for the first time: the sight of so num*
company of serious people affected me. The
cy, propriety, and seriousness, with which the p
ers conducted the meeting, was extremely pl
I was two or three times brought to tear
yet, Satan tempted me not to think, as I ou*
the experience of some who spake, becat
country people related it in so uncouth a n
On coming home, my mother said nothing a*
me, though she knew I had been at the mee

"June 15. My cousin Hopwood and I
this morning to Dring-houses: I believe the
work of grace begun in her heart. Miss
also, who was awakened under Mr. Rich*
seems now to be brought into liberty. I ha*
of late, deeply affected for my dear frien*

Carr, who is severely afflicted with a cancer; yet it is amazing with what composure and sweetness she speaks of death, and of the things of God.

"June 19. I met Mrs. Crosby, an eminently pious woman, of Leeds, at Mrs. Buckle's; she seemed much interested in my welfare, and gave me many instructions, and advised me particularly to pray with simplicity, and to request the Lord to teach me to come to him with all the simplicity of a little child. She desired my good, not only on my own account, but with a view to the good it would prove to others.

"June 28. I awoke this morning very much depressed; the bible was tasteless to me: yet, awhile afterwards, I read a collection of psalms and hymns, for two hours, with a pleasure I scarce ever remember. A hymn, called the Beggar, caused me to weep much, to have it fulfilled in my own case.

'Nor can I willing be,
   Thy bounty to conceal
From others, who, like me,
   Their wants and hunger feel:
I'll tell them of thy mercies' store,
And try to send a thousand more.'

"July 2. While walking to Dring-houses, my mind was in a pleasing frame: the things which once were a weight, in my efforts to give my heart to God, began now to appear as of little moment: I felt a desire to be whatever the Lord would have me be. I afterwards began to repeat the promises, and thereby worked up my mind to a degree of faith and encouragement.

"July 9. This evening I heard Mr. Wesley: his venerable looks inspired me with a veneration for him I cannot express. (July 12.) Mrs. Hall invited me to breakfast with him: I accepted the invitation, and was much pleased to see how this great minister of the gospel conducted himself among plicity.

"July 25, (to 28.) This was a remarkable d[me. Two ladies having advised me to stay mo[home, and read, and meditate, and not go so [to the Methodist chapel, I went embarrasse[Mrs. Hall: she thought I was just where I two months ago: she advised me to get alone take the promises, and put the Lord to his w[and to wrestle with him in prayer, as one reso[not to rise from my knees till I found the bles[of acceptance. I took her advice, and my sp[were exhausted in prayer, being seldom less t[an hour on my knees. It seemed to me a de[rate remedy; but at present, in regard to me failed of effect. However, pleading the prom[furnished me with arguments in prayer. I plea[that God's word had discovered my bondage and sins; that it had brought me the joyful news of li[ty, and invited me to the marriage supper, wher[things were ready: and as the word had brought thither, I pleaded that I never would go till Lord had blessed me: I claimed the blessin[my right through the promises: I put the Lor[his word, and urged my title to be made cl[

unto all them that call upon him.' I won-
that I should think the Lord at a distance.
rayer, I took a walk, and had a delightful
converse and communion with God. Mrs.
vas exceedingly rejoiced at my confidence,
dvised me to continue pleading with the
I now felt myself at the posts of mercy's
nd that all the powers of darkness were not
pluck me thence.
ly 30. This morning, while again pleading
e Almighty to fulfil the word of promise, a
thought darted across my mind, ' Thy
s truth:' immediately such an emanation of
eamed on my soul, as caused me very great
hment and joy; all my faculties seemed
d, and every object seemed to assume a
aspect. I viewed my own righteousness
ing; and earthly objects vanished as chaff
the wind. I spent the whole morning me-
on the treasure opened in my heart; and
us sentiment seemed to succeed another;
ry one of them apparently came from the
f God, because of the lustre and joy that
d them. I continued in this frame till
when my joys seemed to droop in the con-
ns of the day.
g. 10. Having been, for some time, in a
suspense and dejection, not having held
blessing I received awhile ago, I resolved
o repeat Mrs. Hall's advice, and wrestle

ing at my bed-side, I several times repea
determination not to cease crying to him
obtained acceptance: I remained on my
from half-past six in the morning till I
one, only walking about a little to rest my
My mother, on entering my chamber, and
ing the cause, was exceedingly tender to r
fully entered into my sentiments. When
to dinner, the circumstance renewed my
and, unable to act for myself, I threw my so
at the Saviour's feet: the Lord, I trust, he
for, after eating a little, and returning to
he was very gracious to me, and gave
drawings of his love: my heart melted wit
tude for his goodness. These comforts wer
ever, but transient. The rest of the eveni
dull, my body and spirits being much exh
yet a sweet peace rested on my mind.

"Aug. 12. I called on Mrs. Hall. S
very thankful for the mercies that the Lo
shewn me. But on asking her advice, she
modestly excused herself, being wishful to le
wholly in the Lord's hands; afterwards sl
that many would now look upon themse
being in a justified state; yet as I was n
satisfied, she advised me still to wait on th
for a clearer manifestation of his love: she
however, surprised, that I had not held
promise I received a fortnight ago.

"Aug. 19. Having engaged to breakfi
my old friend, Mrs. Burton, I felt the Lo
gracious to me before I went: my soul was
into gratitude and love for all his mercies.

brought to my mind. I find the preaching
. Hunter and Mr. Story of great benefit to
ul.

ct. 10. Yesterday I felt my affections cold
Sacrament; but to-day many texts came
omfort. The love of God was shed abroad
heart. A trial intervened which discomposed
ind; but after some exercises, I felt the love
d stronger and stronger in my heart. Indeed,
so happy, that every doubt and fear seemed
banished. The 103d Psalm I repeated
nd over again: ' Bless the Lord, O my soul,
l that is within me bless his holy name,' &c.

ct. 31. In the middle of the past month,
nd was much harassed with my former doubts
ruples; and I declined a visit to Killingbeck,
e Mrs. Carr thought it best for me to stay at
till I was more established in grace. But
orning, under Mr. Story at the meeting, and
. at the church, I was melted with grateful
yes; all my affections were softened by the
f God. My whole frame was humble and
as a little child. I wished for nothing:
ted only to be as the clay in the potter's

ct. 3. My heart was this morning softened

I now think nothing of my understanding
as though I hardly knew any thing at
I desire no knowledge but that which fl
God through Jesus Christ.

"Oct. 6. A friend to-day expressed a
Mrs. Carr should more and more imbibe
of Mysticism, so as to seclude herself fro[m]
till she was fully established. This was a
to me. I had suffered so much from Mys[ticism]
directing me to enter on a high course of
cation before I was justified, that I fear[ed]
friend. However, on seeing Mrs. C. and
time after her sickness, I saw no just gr[ound]
the apprehension; she was, as usual, an op[en]
in the Lord.

"Oct. 23. Mrs. Crosby spent some h[ours]
me to-day, and her conversation was m[ore]
factory than her letters. By reading [of]
MARSHALL, and HERVEY, I had adopted
expressions concerning justification by th[e]
tation of Christ's active, and of his passi[ve]
eousness: [a form of speaking which Z[uinglius]
had introduced into the church.] She
mended me rather to keep to the old ex[pressions]
in the Liturgy, and to ask every thing '
the merits of our Lord and Saviour Jesus
Whatever blessing I wanted, she advise[d]
keep to praying—believing—waiting [till]
power descended into my soul. She said
a view to Miss S. who was present, and n[ot]
fully clear in the sense of acceptance wi[th]
In the afternoon, we drank tea with the
James Stillingfleet, at Mr. ———. His con[versation]
was not less instructive than his exhortati[on]
made many precious remarks, and was
a catholic spirit. He united the gentle[man]
the Christian more completely than an[y]

, I was not less edified. I inquired concern-
oint which had often embarrassed my mind,
might distinguish the operations of God on
l, from the suggestions of the enemy? She
, that the motions and dictates of the Holy
were mostly sudden and explicit. He
ally impels the mind, in cases of caution,
conviction that such a thought is wrong,
at we ought not to pursue it. And, in all
ises, the first impressions are purest; for by
ing with flesh and blood, we obscure the
s of conscience, and the intimations of God's
ill. Hence, in all cases of temptation, we
redouble our applications to the throne of
for wisdom, support, and comfort.

ec. 17. After many distressing scruples about
which had anew perplexed my mind, I re-
to make to God the sacrifices I believed he
d, that no one might stumble at me. A
spotted silk, the gift of Mrs. Burton, I got
per to exchange; and a quantity of lace,
my sister to keep for my nieces. I wished
in such a neat and easy way as might please
d, and in such a way as would be the least
in the world either for gaiety or negligence.
! dress is nothing compared with my wishes

ing of my heart after holiness. A remark of Mr. Hunter's this evening, did me much good. He said that Satan often foiled us, for want of better skill in using our Christian armour. I now felt a conviction that I ought not to desist from hearing the Methodists. As I get a clearer knowledge of their statement of sanctification, I feel a greater desire to experience it in my heart.

"Jan. 7, 1775. This evening my spirits were very low and much depressed. I went to the chapel at seven o'clock, and, on my return, 'the love of God was shed abroad in my heart;' and in such a degree, that my soul was humbled into the dust. The sentiment of my past ingratitude was so strong, that I saw, if the Lord had sent me to hell for it, he would have done me no wrong. I had, indeed, read many Calvinistic books on justification, but I never saw the fulness and freedom of God's pardoning grace in such a light as I now do.

"Jan. 22. Mrs. Wilson called to-day, and gave me an account of Mrs. Carr's death; and how she was supported in her last moments. Considering the edification and delight I used to receive from the conversation of this saint, I was less affected with the stroke than I expected. Her last moments were employed in praise and gratitude to God; and gratitude was the leading excellence of her character. My heart, however, was melted with love by the solemn intelligence; and in this way the Lord was pleased to sanctify it to my soul.

"Jan. 26. I read Mr. Wesley's Plain Account of Christian Perfection. Mr. R. at tea, spoke well of holiness; but his strictures on the way in which the Methodists sought it, had no weight with me. I was, at this time, much impressed with a dream I lately had, which apparently indicated that the Lord called me to join the Methodists, and at other times I thought that this was not his design.

"Jan. 31. I related my experience to Mr.

mfort belonging to it. And he added, proportion as my faith increased in the of sanctification, for which I was looking, nce would gradually become more clear. y approved of my imploring the Lord to y the root from which all my fears and arose.

he evening, my soul was filled with gra- God, and his love was shed abroad in my My sole wish was, that God's will might accomplished in me. Neither cloud nor eemed to interpose between him and my now feel, if I am convinced it is his that I should join the Methodists, that it a matter of indifference; and I do believe is able to give me the blessing of entire tion."

much to be regretted, that good men ten differ about good things; but religion be reproached with obscurity because of es of opinion, more than nature is to be because philosophers have ever been dis- oncerning her operations. Besides, the of entire sanctification is mentioned by as a subject of the most fervent prayer, han of disputation, Eph. iii. 14, &c. v. 23, 24. And Ezekiel, after enumerating ings of the new covenant, adds, "for all ngs will I be inquired of by the house of chap. xxxvi. The Greek word $T\varepsilon\lambda\varepsilon\iota o\varsigma$, $T\varepsilon\lambda\varepsilon\iota o\tau\eta\varsigma$, *perfection;* and $T\varepsilon\lambda\varepsilon\iota o\omega$, *to per- nctify, to consummate,* occur, I think, not fifty times in the New Testament. The $\theta\alpha\iota\rho\omega$, also, in its various forms, very often he terms expressive of sanctification are

not less frequent. Whoever will carefully inc
into the primitive import of these terms, and c
pare it with the sermons of certain divines,
find an evident falling off. Dr. Samuel Ste
says, that " holiness consists in that *purity of* ?
which is the essence of religion; in a revere
fear and sincere love of God; in a cordial de
diligent aim, and sincere endeavour, to mortify
secret corruptions; in a sovereign contempt of
world, when put in competition with another;
in fervent aspirations of the heart after the like
of God, and after the everlasting fruition of hi
heaven." Serm. vol. i. p. 51. 2d ed. 1772. '
is a fine definition of heart-felt religion; bi
leaves the roots of evil uneradicated from the h
Mr. EVANS, in his sermon on *Purity of Heart*,
equally failed of illustrating the force of our
viour's expression. Dr. Watts has a sentence w
I like still less: " The grave is, as it were,
burial-place of many unruly lusts, which have
the dominion over us in life." And if the g
be so efficacious in purifying the body, with 1
face can we object to the *Limbus* of MARTIAL
the purgatory of the Catholics? We see no
priety in the Scripture similies usually adduce
prove the necessity of in-dwelling sin till de
The leprous house could not be cleansed, bu
a removal to an unclean place! so the lepro
sin must go with the body to the grave.
house, then, was never cleansed at all: but s
leprous houses might be cleansed by scraping
wall. Here the house might be infected whil
tenant was pure; whereas, the contrary is the
with the body and soul; the house cannot be de
without the tenant's consent. The simile of
Canaanites dwelling in the land is equally f
for God passed a positive sentence, of expulsic
death, against those nations distinguished b
comparable wickedness; but when the Isra

had made covenants with them, God would not drive them out; so we really allow is the case with in-dwelling sin.

But do not the advocates of a death-purgatory demonstrate their doctrine from the 7th chapter of the epistle to the Romans, where St. Paul says, "I am carnal, sold under sin?" Jerome and Augustine say, that "S. Paulum hîc loqui in persona peccatoris sub lege adhuc gementis." But in their controversial writings they say, that "S. Paulum de seipso loqui, et in persona hominis justi!" Vide Biblia Magna; et August. l. i. retract. c. 23, et l. vi. contra Julian. c. 11. Hieron. l. ii. contra Pelagianos. Then both those fathers were once of opinion, that St. Paul here speaks in the persons of sinners still under the legal yoke. But why did they alter that opinion? I believe they never did change it. But, in the warmth of argument against the Pelagian, who affirmed, that man was born pure, and that good men lived without sin, they merely pressed Rom. vii. and 1 John i. 7, into their arguments, as applicable to the generality of Christians, who confessedly groan beneath the yoke of in-dwelling corruption.

Do the Methodists, then, teach a sinless perfection as attainable in this life? No: they never use the word. They know that they are all weakness and imperfection: they see themselves encompassed about with a cloud of short-comings and defects. Hence the holiest among them has been taught to say,

"Every moment, Lord, I want,
The merit of thy death."

Nevertheless, they do believe, that as the Lord will destroy antichrist in the church by the breath of his mouth, and by the brightness of his coming, so he can, in a moment, destroy the antichrist of inbred corruption; and say to the leprous heart, "I will, be thou clean." Then the soul is filled with the pure love of God, and all mankind. It

D

the will is lost in the will of God. It is
grace that distinguished David by forbe
when he said, "Let Shimei curse!" It
good that distinguished Stephen in mart
when he said, "Lord Jesus, lay not this
their charge." It is the perfect love of S
which made the confessors and martyrs "
the day of crisis," because, as their Master
were they in this world.

Hence I would advise Christian ministe
cautious of ridiculing a doctrine which is t
hope of the saints. It is far safer to exh
regenerate part of an audience to reach for
press toward the mark for the prize of the
calling, God in Christ Jesus. We should g
more diligence on this head, to add to, o
virtue, to virtue knowledge, &c. not onl
a view to a glorious entrance into heave
because there is no state in active life in whi
and the worst of sins, may not again be fo
have some place in the heart.]

Sunday, Feb. 19, Miss Mortimer writes,
morning, at eight o'clock, Mr. Hunter de
an excellent sermon on sanctification.
afternoon, my soul was truly given up to
I could freely and fully surrender all I had
I can truly say, that I did not wish to ret
idol in my heart. Every thought I desire
brought into obedience to Christ. I desired
riches, nor friends, nor any enjoyment, but
came from him. I have, indeed, experience
of the love of God, yet I never felt the p
freely to surrender myself to him as this e
And if I shall see it the will of God to pl
among the Methodists, I feel ready to do h
having no choice of my own. By readir
Wesley's Sermons and Tracts, I find that h

"March 18. Mr. George Story gave Miss Scott and me some very profitable instructions concerning Christian experience. He said, that every seeker of salvation has a considerable degree of faith; and that we should pray for power to exercise that faith, as it increases by exercise. He observed, that there was a direct and a reflex act of faith. The direct act is, when we look to Christ in his promises, and believe in order to receive. The reflex act is, a consciousness of having received the blessing. As to Christian perfection, he said, that the prejudices of many against it arose from their not making the proper distinction between the diabolical and the human nature. The diabolical nature must be destroyed by the power of grace, while the human nature retains its frailties still. Hence we should pray to be wholly sanctified, and that our body, soul, and spirit, may be preserved blameless unto the coming of our Lord Jesus Christ. After this conversation, I felt faith to believe that I should receive this blessing. But, ah! every time I have named it to Mr. ——, I have felt my mind unhinged, by his inveighing so warmly against it.

"March 24. My sister showed me her drawing-room newly furnished. I returned with my soul humbled, and filled with the love of God. I could bless his name, that I had no taste for vanity. My heart, during the evening, continued in the same delightful frame. "What hath the world to equal this!"

"April 4. On Sunday, I had, for the most part, a happy day, and powerfully experienced the love of God in my heart; I had, likewise, a strong persuasion, that I should receive the blessing of sanctification. And this morning, that persuasion returned; I felt power to believe that the Lord would renew and establish me in righteousness.

"April 5. At noon, my heart was melted with the love of God; and I felt a firm persuasion, that I should receive what I was seeking. My whole heart was fervently drawn toward God, and I preferred lying at the Saviour's feet, to the being mistress of all the world. I think I never experienced so strong a degree of faith as now. My heart was exceedingly humbled before God: I have felt the good of Mr. Story's maxim, to exercise faith upon every occasion.

"July 9. For the last two days, I have had a measure of God's love in my heart, and a growing confidence with it, that the Lord will sanctify my soul, and give his lowly mind. Miss —— having solicited me to write down my motives for altering my dress, with a view to read it to a few friends in Hull, I felt disposed to comply with her request.

"Mrs. Hall (and this was the first time she had ever named it,) modestly intimated her wish that I should join the Methodist Society; but supposed that I could not do it while my mother lived. She thought that my soul would prosper more among them, than where I was at present placed. I simply told her of the trials I had undergone from certain persons with whom I met, and that I had often prayed on that subject; but latterly, our meetings having been more profitable, I felt disposed to remain where I was. She encouraged me much still to go on, looking for sanctification; and thought the Lord was preparing me for it, by imparting more light concerning the holy Scriptures.

"July 31. This evening, being weary with walking, I called at Mr. Spence's, not knowing that it was the night on which his class met. They invited me to stay. It was led that night by a young gentleman designated for the bar. His grave and serious address, distinguished by an engaging politeness, made an impression on my mind.

"Miss S. having reproved me for talking too much, I could not but own it a besetting sin, into which I fell unawares. How good and salutary are the admonitions of a friend!

" Aug. 9. My mother accompanied me to Mr. Spence's class! Considering the prejudices under which she has laboured, and the connection of our family with the church, it was evident to me, that nothing but the grace of God could have influenced her heart to attend a meeting of this kind! Mr. Spence said many excellent things. The privileges of the Methodists are truly great.

" Aug. 29. I have lately profited much by hearing Mr. R. on several searching and awakening subjects. This afternoon he explained to us, at Mr. Buckle's, the first chapter of St. Paul's epistle to the Ephesians. Mrs. Jane Benson had talked with me largely on predestination. Her conversation, and this lecture, unhinged my mind. Mrs. B. told me, likewise, that the sacrifices I had made, with regard to dress, proceeded from a legal spirit."

[How happy was the primitive church, in being ignorant of the doctrines of *unconditional* election and reprobation. The controversy which St. Paul waged with the Jews, on the predestination and adoption of " the Gentiles, to be fellow-heirs with the Jews, of the same body, and partakers of God's promise in the gospel by Christ," was innocent in its bearings, and conclusive in its arguments, Eph. iii. 6. The Jews had wholly arrogated this prerogative to themselves; they would not concede it; they pleaded an exclusive right to all the divine favours by covenant, as stated in their Scriptures. " The Lord, said Moses, hath chosen thee to be a peculiar people unto himself, above all the nations that are upon the earth," Deut. xiv. 2. vii. 6. so also Psal. xxxiii. 12. lxxxix. 3. 19. cv. 6. 43. Isa. xli. 8. Against these assumptions St. Paul urged, that " God, from the beginning, had chosen the Gentiles also to salvation, through sanctification of the Spirit, and belief of the truth," 2 Thess. ii. 13. He proves it from the promises, " I will call them my people, which were not my people; and her beloved, which was not beloved," Rom. ix. 25. This covenant of election and reprobation had its conditions. The Jews were broken off, because of unbelief; and the Gentiles stood by faith. The Jew might be grafted in again; and the Gentiles might be cut off. These are the wholesome inferences of our Apostle, Rom. xi. 20. 23. Thus, every covenant that God has made with man, has its conditions, and strikingly so too, see Deut. xxviii. 1. 15. 1 Sam. ii. 30. 1 Chron. xxviii. 9. Hence, God's choosing the Gentiles before the foundation of the world, or choosing them from the beginning by promise, is all the same thing with him, who, calling the things that are not as though they were, said to Abraham, I have made thee a father of many nations, when as yet he had no child. The periods of this choice are, therefore, but a form of speech; and they were highly consoling to the believing Gentiles, whom the Jews regarded as reprobate, and afar off.

What a pity, then, that GOTESCALCUS, in the ninth century, misguided by the darkness of the age, should be the first that broached the appalling doctrine of unconditional election! HINCMARUS, bishop of Rheims, answered him by a collection of passages out of the fathers, demonstrating that predestination was never taken in an ill sense before. GOTESCALCUS was degraded of his priesthood, and beaten with rods; so *Du Pin* states in his *Ecclesiastical History, century ninth.* I recommend persons unsettled in their notions on these points, to read Mr. John Goodwin's Redemption Redeemed; and Mr. Fletcher's Checks to Antinomianism.]

" Sept. 1. This being a fast-day, on account of the war with the American colonies, I acquainted my brother Mortimer with my intention of going one part of the day to the meeting. He then took occasion to speak with greater disapprobation of the Methodists, and against my sacrifices of superfluities of dress, than I had ever heard him do since his return to York.

"Sept. 27. This morning, while engaged in prayer that God, in his gracious wisdom, would turn the many rebukes I received from my friends to my spiritual good, his mercy, in this view, was so set before me, that my heart was filled with his love. The contradictions of my cousin ——, I was enabled to bear with patience. I have experienced good from Mrs. Hall's class, and from Chappelle's, which I have attended in an accidental way. I new begin to find a confidence that the Lord will establish my soul in righteousness; and I feel a growing attachmentt o the Methodists. But, ah! the trials through which I pass, and my besetment of talking too much, often throw me back into discouragements and temptation.

"Oct. 14. Having received a friendly invitation from Miss Brooke, I prepared to visit the family at Killingbeck. On my return, I began to reflect what good I had done, what errors I had committed, and what improvements I had made. I had related my experience to Miss B. with a view to encourage her in the good way; and I had profited by reading; but by paying and receiving visits with the family, levity, my old besetting sin, had frequently gained the ascendency over me.

"Dec. 3. For some time my mind has been variously exercised. Since my return from K, I have seriously endeavoured to combat my propensity to levity and fondness of talk. I have seldom reflected on a tea-party, but some shade of reproach has rested on my mind on this account. On the other hand, my friends wonder at my gravity; and some of my family behave rather haughtily to me in respect of dress: well, it all drives me to a nearer union with God, and with his people. Mrs. W. and I have had some conversation, and she has directed us on what plan to form a little class. Mr. R. called also: he was more open than usual. With regard to me, he said, that he should say no more with regard to doctrines, Methodism, &c. for he saw that it had the contrary effect of his intentions; and he said this with much affection. Yes, I must persevere in whatever I see to be my call and line of duty; and I would in no case take a step in haste, when it is a doubtful matter.

" Dec. 7. I have felt my soul much blessed at the morning prayer while in the church; and very much edified while at Mr. Spence's class. Whenever I do not find the love of God in my heart, I am fully resolved to examine the cause, and to have it removed. I begin to feel more and more a spirit of intercession for the church, and union and communion with God in all the means of grace, and my soul is humbled by his goodness.

" Jan. 8, 1776. This year has opened to me with a series of trials. I am reproached with being more attached to the Methodists than to the church; I am tried with a friend who has formed a connection with one who, I think, has not experienced a change of heart; I am tried also with another dear friend who is enslaved by the fear of man; and, I lament to add, that these trials discover the latent corruptions of my own heart. Thank God, when I get into his house, and look above them all, my soul is favoured with his presence and love.

" Jan. 11. Mr. —, forgetful of his promise, lent me a book on imputed righteousness. I have no doubt of my Redeemer's merits, which I make my only plea, but dislike the refinements of Zuinglius, so admired by Mr. Hervey. I have too long been hampered by a two inactive faith of reliance; I want the simple faith of a little child, that I may daily come to my heavenly Father, and at once receive the bread of heaven." [If our guilt is removed by the passive righteousness of Christ, and if our persons be justified by the imputation of his active righteousness, we must be all equally righteous; and, consequently, can have no need of that *third* righteousness so constantly enforced by St. Paul, the being created anew in righteousness and true holiness; and having all the fruits of the Spirit, which are, love, joy, peace, *righteousness*, faith, &c.]

" I received a kind letter from Miss Bosanquet, (now widow of the late Rev. Mr. Fletcher) chiefly on sanctification : it proved exceedingly profitable; every sentence seemed a portion of meat for my soul; and it enlarged my heart in prayer to obtain the blessing.

" Jan. 18. Our old and gay circle of friends were this evening preparing for festivity, to celebrate the queen's birth-day : to us it was a night of mourning. I went to sit up with my sister Mortimer, but was prevented by the stroke of death. I was much depressed that I had not been more faithful with her about her soul. Ah! death has now settled all the arguments we have held together on gaiety and dress ! She has now no need of all the improvements lately made in her drawing-room, &c. My brother was deeply affected : I never saw him half so much distressed in all my life.

" Jan. 23. During the hurry of the funeral, I found it difficult to keep my mind where it ought to be; and I felt the want of secret prayer. My mother spent the evening with my brother. I was engaged in other duties. He lamented the way in which I was, as it precluded my being useful to him, and to his children, in the way that I might. Lady Anderson, and Mr. Bewley, joined him in what he said; and, when my mother told me what had passed, I felt not the least displeasure against them: four days afterward I breakfasted with him, and solicited to take two of the children. He was rather warm, and said, that I should turn Molly a Methodist.

"On the occasion of my sister's death, I resolved to write to my brother, at Oxford, about his soul: I did so, and with great freedom: I felt not the least fear of offending him; nor any bias from the advantages I might reap in future from his favour. I retired to my chamber at night with a placid conscience, and happy in God. I felt grateful to God, on looking over my sister's dresses, that they had made no impression on my heart: my faith enabled me to rise above the vanities of life. Lord, it is thy grace which has made the difference.

"March 1. Mr. R. observed a sort of anniversary in our meeting. Instead of expounding a passage of scripture, he proceeded, after prayer, to admonish his people of eight faults he had noticed in the preceding year: his manner was solemn and instructive. 1. Indulging evil surmising against one another, which were the result of pride. 2. A love of gossipping. 3. The not being always employed. 4. The being Christians in public, and not so in our families. 5. A love of talking, and fondness of religious news. 6. A love of self-esteem, discovered by a propensity to speak of ourselves. 7. A fondness of giving our advice and opinion. 8. A passionate or peevish temper, which made us very unlike our gentle master. There was another fault mentioned, by the bye, that is, religious gossipping from one ordinance to another, which could not be so profitable as meditation and prayer at home. This I considered as pointed directly at me: but I was not condemned, being conscious of the good I had received from the Methodist ministry, and from an occasional attendance on their class-meetings.

"March 27. Rising this morning in an uneasy frame of mind, I spent a long time in prayer with God, because I had felt an unwillingness to pray; and I have often had thus to plead with God, and it never fails to restore me to composure of mind. How thankful should I be for this resource! It draws my mind from earthly things, that it may be stayed on God alone. It enables me to reject obtrusive thoughts, and excites my faith to a lively confidence in the Lord. For the most part, I spend an hour and a half in prayer every morning, allowing for intervals in which I rest my knees. The flesh often complains, and is reluctant; but I always find it best to spend the whole of the morning before breakfast in reading, and in communion with God.

" March 30. Mrs. Wilson took breakfast with me; her conversation was very profitable: she remarked, that we must often examine ourselves, as to what keeps us out of the blessing we want, and, by so doing, the blessing is brought nearer: by not wrestling with God for this, we often misimprove the opportunities which God affords. Watchfulness, joined to prayer, is most assuredly the happiest means to retain and enjoy the abiding witness of the Holy Spirit; and I am resolved to practise it more than ever.

" April 3. Mr. Hilton took tea with us. He endeavoured to convince my mother, that she laboured under religious prejudices, in not attending the preaching, and class-meetings; and he observed, among other things, that when live coals are put together, the fire burns vehemently; but, when the coals are scattered, the fire dies away. He observed farther, that God has enjoined us not to forsake the assembling of ourselves together, and that we have no more right to violate this precept than any other; consequently, the Spirit can never lead us secretly to act contrary to his revealed will. Nay, he gave a decided preference to being guided by the written word, as the finger post which directs the traveller in his route. For instance, he added, the Quakers disuse the holy sacrament altogether, and affirm, that they are guided so to do by the Spirit. We, on the contrary, think it right to celebrate this ordinance till the Lord shall come.

How are we to determine this point but by the written word? I have always remarked, that this preacher's conversation turns on profitable subjects, and is exceedingly instructive and profitable. He is the same in the pulpit: his sermons are close and searching.

"April 10. My morning meditation, on our Saviour's transfiguration, was very profitable to me. The testimony of the Father, "This is my beloved Son, in whom I am well pleased," afforded abundance of consolation to my soul. I had, in the evening, likewise, much communion with God. I was often constrained to exclaim, O! the length, the breadth, the depth, and height, of the love of Christ, which passeth knowledge! I had a most impressive sense of the emptiness of my own wisdom. I was humbled by a view of the purity of God, and I desired to be wholly guided by his Spirit. Every thing in me appeared to be vile, and unworthy of divine regard. But, ah! levity, my daily besetting sin, often gains a degree of ascendency over me, and leaves a dissatisfaction whenever I retire from company.

"April 30. To-day Mr. — asked me my experience more closely than usual, adding withal, that I seemed to talk more of myself than of Christ. Presuming on his apprehensions, that I rested on frames and feelings, I simply told him my whole heart, and assured him, that it was a view of the wisdom, goodness, and love of God, that often occasioned my heart to glow with divine affection. I added, that I knew of no other way of acquiring a consciousness of adoption, or of his Spirit bearing witness of it to my spirit, than by the love of God shed abroad in my heart, arising from a view of his love to me; and that, when I did not feel that peace and joy, but, on the contrary, felt my corruptions uppermost, it was solely by beholding the merits of my Redeemer, that consolation was restored to my soul.

"Since this conversation with Mr. R. I have seen more clearly than ever the error of those who decry frames and feelings. Assuredly, there can be no genuine peace and joy felt in the heart, and which always humble the soul, but what arise from beholding the glory of the Lord, and the excellency of our God: hence, if my heart is filled with love, whether it be by hearing the glory of my Redeemer set forth in a sermon, or by reading and meditation, it is so far, in my opinion, from resting in frames and feelings, that it is rather an evidence of my having the true faith, which produces those consolations in my heart. Mr. R. seemed perfectly satisfied with what I had said; yet, all I said to him, in favour of the Methodists, seemed to make no lasting impression on his mind. I agree with him, however, that I have been injudicious, in grieving my mother by applauding them; and yet I could not be silent when I heard them misrepresented.

"June 4. This evening I was much edified at Mrs. Hall's class: she said, a Christian should always be receiving from the fulness of God, and returning what he gave in praise and thanksgiving: If we did not return, she said, what he gave us, in grateful acknowledgments, we should become offensive as the stagnant waters. She described the barren faith, which did not produce the fruits of the Spirit, and exhorted us to get every Christian temper and affection formed in the heart. She remarked, that it was quite a mistake to suppose, that we were growing in grace, unless we had an increase of faith, and love, and meekness, and resignation.

"June 14. Last evening I walked with my mother, and, on passing the Methodist chapel, it came into my mind to ask her to go in, and character of his diciples, "Ye are the salt of the earth." Miss Ritchie's conversation and manner were so truly christian, that, while I was in her company, and for some time afterwards, I seemed to feel as though I had hardly any religion, or had attained any experience. They ask a blessing at tea, and do every thing with a simplicity and grace resembling heaven.

"From conversations so instructive, I can but select a few fragments, which may be of use to me at another day; and with that view I treasure them up in my journal.

"In one conversation Mr. Wesley remarked, that if we see the blessing we seek at a distance, it will always remain so, unless we make continual efforts to attain it.

"When we feel our faith weak and low, we resemble the man with the withered hand, and then is the time to stretch it forth, for the Lord is always present to heal.

"It is wrong to expect the power before we believe; we should believe in order to receive the power, just as the little child keeps making effort to walk, till he can walk.

"Love, joy, and peace, are the fruits, not the foundation, of this faith.

"Mr. Cornelius Caley observed, that when we are most tempted, that was often the time when the Lord was about to give us a blessing.

"The Lord often grants us blessings in a way which we think the most likely to counteract them. In outward providences, we often walk in darkness, and have no light; but, by trusting in the Lord, he often exceeds our expectations.

"Instead of wasting our time in reasonings, and in groundless scruples, we should direct all our efforts to believe, and look to the cross of Christ to be healed of every wound.

"While we are seeking after holiness, the evidences of our justification will become clearer and clearer; for the desire of holiness is a present blessing. Our constant prayer should be, Lord, enable me, this day, to embrace thy will.

"After tea I went with Miss Ritchie to meet Mrs. Hall's class. It was, indeed, a very edifying opportunity. I was struck with the simplicity and grace with which she conducted herself through the whole of this exercise. The image of God, formed in her soul, seemed to shine forth in her prayer and conversation with the people. During all the time I have been with her, I have never noticed any thing contrary to the sanctification she professes to enjoy. She excels in pressing the people to look for higher degrees of grace: every person who was awakened, she pressed to look for justification; and every one who is justified, she exhorted to look for a clear evidence of sanctifying grace. She really is a very extraordinary person; the more I become acquainted with her, the more she rises in my affection and esteem. If Mr. R. with whom she has had frequent conversations, would invite her to meet his people, she would be

"July 31. Miss Ritchie and I had some conversation respecting my joining the Methodist society. Having long met in class with Mrs. Hall, I told her that I had often made it a matter of prayer. I acknowledged to her that they were more alive to God than Mr. R.'s people, as I had done to Mr. Hilton, (April 12,) and that he had asked me the same question which she had just put, viz. In what way I expected an answer to my prayer? If the people were more lively; and if I had a prospect of being more holy and useful, he thought these strong indications of the will of God. I told her I had acknowledged to him, that the cross was one great hinderance, for I feared the resentment of my mother and friends: besides, I thought it would involve me in a separation from Mr. R. Miss Ritchie saw no occasion for this; for I might continue to meet with both, as I had been accustomed to do. I replied, that, as the Lord had led me to adopt the principles of the Methodists, and to admire their discipline, I had gradually made up my mind to join them, whenever I could find liberty and resolution to do it. She approved of my plan, and advised me to continue praying, that I might be faithful to the light which God might give me.

"Walking out with my mother before dinner, but without any previous design, I simply told her, that I had latterly entertained serious thoughts of joining the Methodists. She seemed much hurt, and not a little agitated. Mr. R. called in the afternoon, and the first word with my mother was, to apprise him of my intention. He behaved better on the occasion than I expected, though it was evident enough he was decidedly against it; for he took up the subject as though it had already been done.

"Jan. 1, 1777. This morning I spent an hour in prayer, and carefully endeavoured to review my infirmities, defects, and sins, during the past year.

avoured also to make an estimate of my
s, that I might be the more grateful and
it. My habit is irritable, and I have often
vercome with levity, and a too great fond-
talk. My soul has often been very happy
love of God; yet I have attained neither the
witness of God's Spirit, nor the grace of
cation, for which I have so often wrestled
iod. I seem, however, for the future, re-
to live to God for the present moment.
b. 16. Towards the close of this week, I
nced much dissatisfaction with myself, in
to the small progress I had made in van-
ig my besetting sin; yet I have had many
able visits of God's love. The spirit of
has also been abundantly given me for
—, who was much on my mind, that the
ould make him more clear with regard to
y of salvation in his preaching, and that he
feed the flock committed to his care: I
likewise, that he and the Methodists might
closer union. For several others of my
is friends I have also been led to pray, with
ervour of mind.

ever, I feel, has resulted from those pleadings
God in which I have been engaged, it has le
to feel and experience the nature of faith
clearly than ever, both in regard of comm
with God, and of reliance on the promises.

"While thus led on, and seeking puri
heart, Mrs. Crosby took breakfast with me
dropped me many judicious hints. She
proved of my spending so much time in p
as it interfered with other duties of life;
though it was our duty to be ever reaching
for more of God, yet believers found the bl
of sanctification at different periods of life.
whole conversation was very instructive and
table. She lives in the spirit of doing good.

"Oct. 9. Yesterday my cousin Hopwoo
married to Mr. Grey.* On a calm review o
family occurrence, I have, from a variety of
dences, abundant reason to believe, that the
is of the Lord. Notwithstanding all their
cautions of secrecy, many of their religious fi
found their way to the church, and there

* William Grey, Esq. of the City of York, Solici
extensively known, he having long held the office of
Sheriff of the country. Mrs Pawson's augurs concerni
gentleman have been more than realized, both in his r
character, and in his professional duties.

joined with their good wishes and fervent prayers. I prayed for them both very fervently in secret; and, likewise, for the prosperity of the church, and, especially, that all divisions may be healed, and the party-spirit destroyed, and that we might love as brethren, notwithstanding the variation in religious opinions. But, oh! when shall this prayer be answered! when shall so many devout and pious persons learn to show the same compassion to one another's peculiar tenets, that they do to their mental and bodily infirmities!

"Oct. 22. I drank tea to-day with Mr. and Mrs. Chapel, and stayed at the class, which meets in their house. His conversation was very profitable. If those with whom we visit are not of use to us, we should always endeavour to be of use to them. He was of opinion, that the Lord had, in a great measure, sanctified my soul, and that I ought to exert faith in the promises concerning this work, saying, "Lord, I believe, help thou my unbelief." He observed, that those who were in that happy state, could mostly draw from God, by a single aspiration, whatever they needed; while those, who lived below their privilege, had to obtain it by repeated efforts of prayer. This pious and holy man is a local preacher in Mr. Wesley's connexion, and of good report. I never leave his house without a savour of good things.

"Jan. 1, 1778. Having ended the year happy in God, I propose to set out afresh, and to re-double my vigilance against the evils which have beset me. I mean, every evening, to examine myself with regard to the defects of the day, and endeavour to amend them for the future.

"Feb. 1. This evening I attended the select band of the Methodists, at Thomas Chapel's, and found it very profitable. It consists of persons who either enjoy the abiding witness of God's love, or who profess to be seeking entire sanctification. I have also been much blessed in reading the life of Francis Xavier, the far-famed apostle of the Indies: my soul longed to imitate him in devotion. The conversation of Mrs. Hall has likewise proved very edifying to me. When persons are first justified, she observed, they might have much joy, but it was not that pure and humble joy which they attain on arriving at a higher degree of grace. The first is mixed with much of nature, and soon lost in the time of temptation; but the love and joy they afterwards receive, is like 'the little leaven that leaveneth the whole lump.' I was three years, she added, in learning to say, ' Thy will be done;' and I have still to learn.

"April 17. Having, on Sunday last, felt much enlargement in prayer, while at church, for Mr. R. and his people, and, in particular, for Lady Anderson, I waited on her to-day, and found much freedom in talking to her of the state of her soul. She heard me with attention, but put it off in too light a way to afford me satisfaction.

"March 3. Mrs. H. reproved me to-day, for seeking knowledge more than grace. My pride was wounded by the rebuke, because it was given in the presence of several persons, who apparently approved of what was said. I went home in humility and silence, praying that I might profit by it, and that all undue wishes to have the good for devotion, God is set before us; and the spirit in which they were written, imperceptibly steals upon us.

"In the evening, I attended the select band, with a mind unhinged, from having talked too much in the day. Mr. C. after speaking his experience, superadded several excellent things. He magnified the power of grace, and said, that it was impossible to live to God for a single moment, unless we were divinely kept by the power of God; that we are not sufficient of ourselves to think a gracious thought; and that our greatest hindrance in the attainment of sanctification is, the not giving up our will in all things to the Lord. Mrs. Hall spoke next, of the necessity of living to God for the present moment; and of our constant need of fresh supplies of grace. She enlarged on the privileges of a clean heart, that we may run the ways of God's commandments. On this subject, she felt at home; and the simplicity and power with which she spake, seemed to overshadow the whole of the people. My soul was truly refreshed, and overflowed with gratitude to God, for permitting me to meet with his people. O, how great are their privileges!

"May 18. I mourned to-day for the want of watchfulness, in not having my conversation seasoned with grace. I had given way to sharpness of spirit. In the afternoon, I met a party of religious friends at Mrs. Buckle's. Dr. Osmond edified us with many excellent remarks. Speaking of justification, he said, that in all sincere seekers, unbelief was the principal sin to be convinced of; that when properly convinced of this, we should say to them, 'Come, for all things are now ready.' His remarks on sanctification, I thought very valuable. Miss H. asked, whether a person in that state had still need of the atonement. Assuredly, he replied, they need it every moment, and they have it every moment; therefore they

walk at liberty, and in the light of God's coun
tenance.

"May 14. Miss Ritchie, being on a visit t[o]
York, breakfasted with me this morning. I opene[d]
all my heart to her, with regard to my besetment
and defects, and my method of seeking sanctification
She approved of the way I took, but added, tha[t]
in her own class, she never pressed sanctificatio[n]
on any one in a justified state, till she first hear[d]
some complaint of the corruptions of the hear[t]
Then she could do it with more effect.

"Nov. 9. During the last three months, m[y]
soul has been gaining a little ground in the goo[d]
way. I have daily been more happy, and foun[d]
a greater nearness to God. Sometimes I hav[e]
thought that I enjoy the blessing of sanctification
but a self-will often rising, has discouraged m[e]
from holding fast my confidence. Yet, when m[y]
brother M. has spoken somewhat bitterly agains[t]
the Methodists, it has not hurt me as it used to do
and I have found great power in praying for him
Yesterday, I wrestled hard for the blessing; an[d]
this morning, breakfasting with Mrs. Buckle an[d]
Mrs. Hall, my soul was stirred up anew to see[k]
after it. During the conversation, Mrs. Ha[ll]

Saviour's promise for the attainment of sanctification: 'If any man love me, my Father will love him, and we will come unto him, and make our abode with him.' This letter shewed me the path in which I ought to walk, and the method I ought to pursue.

" March 3, 1779. Last night, my dear friend and faithful adviser, Mrs. Bathsheba Hall, died in the Lord. I did not know the time of her death; but about nine o'clock, I found an out-pouring of the spirit of prayer for the whole family, and it occurred to me, that she was probably dead, as it afterwards proved.

" March 5. This day I have attended the remains of Mrs. Hall to the grave; and heard her funeral sermon at the Methodist chapel, by Mr. Thomas Hanson. His text was, ' Then shall the righteous shine forth as the sun in the kingdom of their Father,' Matt. xiii. 43. O, what solemnity! What tears! What power attended the word! I never heard such a funeral sermon before. But words cannot utter the unity and love which subsist among the children of God!

March 7. Mr. Richardson preached to-day on the fear of man. It was, indeed, a sermon to me. On going home, I took the opportunity of opening my whole heart to my mother. I told her plainly, that after going among the Methodists for eight years, keeping close all that time to Mr. R. and to his private meetings, I had long seen it my duty to cast in my lot with that poor despised people; but that I had forborne, lest I should grieve her in old age. She seemed less violent than I expected; but she was still decided against the measure.

" March 19. The Rev. Mr. Collins has been in York for more than a week. I have heard him often. This evening, he delivered a powerful sermon from the 17th chapter of the Second Book of Kings. I was very happy under his word.*

* This gentleman is revered by myriads in the religious world.

"May 5. Mr. Wesley is now here; and he delivered three excellent sermons. In illustra our Saviour's words, ' the blade, the ear, and full corn,' he associated them with St. John's t states of grace, distinguished by children, yo men, and fathers. In explaining Heb. xii. 1 warned the people against what are called things, such as a positive temper, which affec be always in the right; and its opposite, a v and pliable temper; rudeness, sternness, and needless indulgences of snuff and tobacco. In first sermon, on 1 Cor. xiv. 20, he shewed v reason could do in religion, and what it could do: how far it could carry Socrates, Adrian emperor, &c.; and how far their hope fell sho the Christian's hope; for reason is unable to duce the faith, the hope, and love of a Christia

"This forenoon, Mr. Wesley met the so band: he permitted me to meet, without asl me to join the society. On my return, I felt g

He was curate, a while, at Roade, near Frome; afterwar Lowgate, in Hull. Here his popularity was so great, tha vicar, and some other gentlemen, piqued at the warmth young convert, dismissed him. About five thousand pe attended him on the quay, while he preached, prior to his lea the town. And, if we may except the short labours of Mr. F that church has exhibited the gloom of an almost forsaken ten

On leaving Hull, he cast himself on the care of Provide and continued to make journeys throughout the United King and to preach in all churches, chapels, &c. where a door opened. Gentlemen, who knew his life and labours, more supplied all his wants: and he was the faithful almoner o the surplus to the poor. Wishful to be a faithful steward, to repress his natural propensity to pride, he placed his fa in the humblest cottage of Tiverton, near Bath. The rent forty shillings per annum; and the broken beam was suppo by the knotty end of an oak pole in the middle of the h Yet Mr. Collins was a man of polished manners, a schol high classical taste, and a Christian of distinguished simpl

...rd will either make my way, or give me grace break through. I feel much satisfaction, that it now generally known to Mr. R.'s people, that y mother is the sole hindrance of my joining the ethodists.

"May 8. Yesterday Mrs. Buckle called to say, at Mr. Wesley, in calling over the names of the lect band, had (some one inadvertently answering r me,) put down my name: but as it was only in e band, and as I was not joined in any class, it is quite optional, she said, whether I would let it ind. I felt thankful that the Lord had so far ide my way, and without my own will. I there- re sat down this morning, and wrote to Mr. R. inform him of my intention to join the Me- odists, as soon as opportunity offered; that as ey already looked upon me as one of the society, om my long attendance on the select band, I did t see it right to retract. I alleged the great od I had found among the Methodists, and odestly hinted at the pain I felt, that many of ose who attended his meeting, should so much nform to the world in dress, &c.; and that all y talking to them on that head had no effect, but emed to ruffle their temper. Nevertheless, I ded, if they would still permit me to meet among em, that I should account it an honour to wash eir feet.

"After writing this letter, I felt much peace in my n soul, and a spirit of prayer for Mr. R. and his ople. And I have the more cause to be thankful, it little danger is to be apprehended from my ther. She seems now to leave me to my own

nature was ready to revolt, and unwilling to rece
the blessing from it which Providence design
One complained of a difficulty in the introduct
of religious conversation; and Mrs. C. replied, t
when a few religious people meet for edification,
was obviously our duty to change the conversat
to the wishes of the party.

"Sept. 10. I have enjoyed to-day a meas
of the love of God shed abroad in my heart, wh
has been my daily privilege for some time p;
But I was pained at feeling a degree of pride
myself, and impatience with my mother, who tc
the word out of my mouth, when speaking
a person, and did not, I thought, speak so mt
to the point as I had intended to do.

"Breakfasting with Mr. Hunter, I took 1
liberty of asking the import of a conversation
had with a clergyman some years ago, which,
that time, I did not understand. The gentlem;
he answered, contended, that a believer must alwa
come to God as a guilty sinner. This, he sa
was wrong, unless we have contracted some fre

guilt; for there is no condemnation to them that are in Christ Jesus. Yet we need the atonement every moment, to take away our defects.

"Jan. 1, 1780. To-day I felt a strong desire to begin afresh, and follow on to know the Lord. Mr. Fenwick gave us a suitable discourse, on forgetting the things behind, and reaching forth to those that are before. I saw it my calling to be free from all inordinate attachment to the creature, and wholly the Lord's. I have often felt a spirit of prayer for the abiding witness, of intercession for the church, which has usually been followed by a spirit of praise and thanksgiving. I daily see, more and more, that my growth in every Christian temper, must be proportioned to my growth in faith and love.

"April 7. To-day, as in general, I enjoyed a sense of God's love, and felt a cry in my heart that it might increase more and more. I felt a hungering and thirsting after righteousness, and the abiding Comforter. I regarded my inordinate thirst after knowledge, as hurtful to my growth in grace. I read too many books, and often lay them aside before I have read them through. I have found no books better to my soul than the Bible, and Mr. Wesley's extract of the Life of De Renty, and of Kempis on the Imitation of Jesus Christ. Miss Raison lately was so frank as to apprise me, that the frequent hurry of my spirits was a hindrance of my growth in grace. How good is it to have a faithful friend, to admonish us of our daily defects! The character of Martha, rather than of Mary, has been mine. I want the habits of holiness, to retain the good I receive.

"June 20. This morning, Mrs. Wilson, Esther Chapel, Ruth Hall, Miss Raison, and myself, began a band-meeting. I felt much love for Mrs. Wilson, who led it; I hope it will prove a blessing to us all. In the evening, I sat down and took a calm review of my heart and character. I saw curiosity, and a fondness of meddling with thing I had no business with, had captivated me. Bu that my ruling passion had been pride, connecte with vanity, and a love of company. And, to sa all in one word, what must the root of all the propensities be but devilish! Yet I have pleade with the Lord, for an hour together, for sanctifyin grace.

"Dec. 21. This day, after gaining my mother consent, and spending some time with her in praye I went to Mr. Thomas Taylor, and joined th Methodist society. I had written a second tim to Mr. R. to permit me still to meet with h people; but whether he will consent, I know not.

"March 6, 1781. This day my dear moth finished her mortal course, and I have been da and night so closely confined, as to neglect m journal. My dear parent, long worn down wit an obstinate asthma and cough, began to alter i her health on the 23d of February, and daily afte to grow worse and worse. I wrestled with Go for her about two hours, that she might hav a clear evidence; and the evening before she die I prayed from ten till three in the morning, tha the Lord would finish his work in her soul, an cut it short in righteousness.

"During the eleven days of her severer sicknes there was a remarkable change in her. She aj peared as a child, and had nothing in her hea but love to God and man, having given all thing up into the Lord's hands. At one time, when w thought her dying, she revived, and said, 'M soul is returning home to God.' She said,

Lucy's coming in, she said, "My dear, I am glad to see you; the Lord is in this place:" she added, "I hope you will all take occasion to thank the Lord on my account: I die in the faith, and have no doubt that the Lord will save me." Then, turning her eyes towards Lucy, she said, "Look at me, and turn from the world." She then repeated our Saviour's words, "My peace I leave with you; my peace I give unto you:" so she fell asleep in Jesus. O what an argument of holiness and diligence, is the idea of a parent, and so many dear friends, in glory! Thank God, my mind has been more supported than I could have expected, considering the greatness of my loss: and the Lord has wonderfully opened the heart of my brother Mortimer to me: he has added about 30l. per annum more to my income, besides soliciting the kindness of my brother Timothy.

"April 2. Since my mother's death, my mind has been much drawn to prayer; and, whatever station in life his Providence may call me to, shall be for the best. I have been much profited by reading Miss Bosanquet's tract on "Jesus altogether Lovely; or, the Advantages of a Single Life." At church and sacrament I found a great desire to be wholly given up to God. The sermons, also, of Mr. Thomas, and Mr. Joseph Taylor, are made a blessing to me whenever I hear them.

"Aug. 1. To-day I received a letter from my brother Mortimer, containing the gratifying intelligence, that he was unanimously chosen Rector, or head, of Lincoln college, Oxford. I hope his preferment will not lift him up. My soul has often been engaged with God, on his account, for an hour together.

"Oct. 13. For the last two months I have been much engaged with God for a clean heart: I have cried earnestly that pride, self-love, and impatience, might be all destroyed; and, during my conflicts for the blessing, and besetments from Mr. ———;

I have had many encouraging promises from the Lord, and much help from my friend Ruth Hall; and this morning, after a little struggle, many promises came, with much of life and love, that the Lord had made me clean: in a short time after, many other promises came to my mind, that the Lord would seal me his to the day of redemption.

"Oct. 27. For the last fortnight I have had many conflicts with the enemy: he endeavours to shake my confidence, and often to bring the creature to my mind, either in a painful, or a pleasing way. One day I called and opened all my state to R. Hall. She wished me much to hold fast my confidence, that the Lord had sealed me by his Spirit. By acting faith upon the promises, she observed, the light would grow clearer and clearer. On my return, I was thinking of her advice, and these words came to my mind, " Once have I heard, and twice hath God spoken, that power belongeth unto God: also, " whatsoever ye desire in prayer, believe that ye receive it." It occurred likewise to my mind, that, at intervals, when free from the power of temptation, I often found the Lord shining on my soul, as though the work was done, and, consequently, that I had but to keep up that exercise of faith, for the light to shine clearer and clearer still.

" Dec. 15. My journal has been neglected; but the work of grace has been gradually going forward in my soul, and the enemy has had less power to tempt me. The Lord seems teaching me to depend wholly on himself, and on the guidance of his counsel. Mr. Thomas Taylor has lately appointed me to meet a band; and I feel great pleasure that Mrs. Preston has at length consented to meet with me.

" Jan. 9, 1782. A circumstance, on Wednesday last, surprised me not a little; it was an offer of marriage from the Rev. Mr. Wren, one of Lady Huntington's preachers: he told me, that, from the first time of seeing me at ———, about twenty months ago, I had been often brought to his mind. We had casually met together, two or three times, when visiting the sick; but I had not the most distant idea of his thinking of me, as we were of different opinions in religion, and belonged to different denominations. I totally declined his overtures; though he was not wanting to press the sphere of usefulness it would open to me.

"Jan. 16. Mr. Wren has called twice; but I have persisted to deny him, and with the greatest composure. He has made a friend of Mr. Parker [a barrister] to urge his suit.

"Feb. 1. Mr. Wren called to-day, and stayed at tea. When he was gone, I retired for three hours and a half, and laid the affair before the Lord, that I might either decline his offer altogether, or let it go on.

"Feb. 2. After praying to the Lord for direction in this important affair, I cannot encourage Mr. W. though he calls daily, because the matter is not clear to me.

"March 2. My journal has been neglected for a month, during which time the affair with Mr. Wren has been decided for me to give it up, much to his dissatisfaction: he persists in saying, that I have acted under the advice of man, and not the counsel of God. But Mr. Walker, a particular friend of Mr. Wren's, called to-day, and said, that Mr. W. was ill, and charged me with giving encouragement to him, if not in word, at least in action, by allowing him to come so frequently to the house. This I could not deny; but my affections were not entangled; I felt no desire to change: my conscience, however, is somewhat delicately circumstanced; I would neither injure his health, nor wound religion.

"April 8. A spirit of prayer was poured upon me, with abundance of love for several of my religious friends, who have been very severe upon me in this affair: yes, I felt such a flame of love for all my enemies, that I could have done any thing f their good; and God spread a table for me in t midst of them all." [Eight pages are here cut o of the journal.]

"Sept. 14. My journal has been long ne lected; but this day I was married to Mr. Wre I could not see my way to give the connection u] so I leave the issues with the Lord.

"Nov. 21. I have thought, that to be ful united in spirit to my husband, I ought to uni in church fellowship with him; hence, I wrote note to Mrs. Pawson, signifying my intention withdrawing from the Methodists; though I d not know that Mr. Wren intended proposing n as a member, that evening, to his church: neve theless, I found a spirit of prayer for the Meth dists, as I esteemed them in the Lord.

"March 2, 1782. I wrestled to know wher fore the Lord contended with me. A severe tri now exercised my mind. For some time my tria have been great; and corruptions have been di covered in my heart which I never knew befor The Lord seems to sit upon my heart as a refinir fire. My trials proceed from the nearest quartei but I have spent most of three days in prayer f(Mr. Wren and myself.

"June 11. My journal has been neglected f(some months, during which I have been much i the fire; and for the two last days a great weigl has been on my spirits. The Lord seems to she me, that every trial has been but a just punisl ment for my sins. Every thing that I had done f displease the Lord apparently passed before m and a sense of guilt seemed to attend the sigh My only plea was, that Jesus Christ is my adv(cate and intercessor. This morning, however, tl Lord broke in upon my soul, and made me happ in his love.

"Sept. 25. Since July, many severe exercis(have been my portion. Satan has sifted me

ems as paternal corrections, levelled at my
ng sins. Thank God, I have often had the
of prayer; and I see my calling is, to be
; to be as nothing in the eyes of God and

)ct. 18. During the last month, my frames
nd have been various. I have often a deep
of my unworthiness, and regard my trials as
:d at my pride. My cry has been, not only
rdon, but to feel the cleansing power of the
ur's blood, and to be one with him, as
bed John xvii. 21. One day, when wrest-
vith the Lord, those words seemed to dart a
f light through the cloud, " I will chastise
and let him go."
)ct. 27. The Lord gave me a very impressive
ction of my having gone out of the divine
, and my whole cry was for pardon, that he
l once more set my feet upon the rock, and
ish my goings.' Since I disobeyed the Lord,
thing has apparently gone wrong, and every
has seemed to be against me. I have com-
my situation to the disciples in the ship,
Jesus was not with them. My way is dark
enighted: I grope at noon, and stumble at
step. It is true, the spirit of adoption has
left me wholly alone; I could still come to

him; and his presence makes the brightest
yet my cross is still the same; only I can l
better. Mr. Walker, and others of Mr. V
people, are severe upon me for my attachm
the Methodists. I seem called to be silent,
commit my cause unto the Lord.

"Jan. 1, 1784. I still pass through deep v
where there is no standing; but the spirit of p
has rested upon me all the day. My brother
I am told, a little softened towards me: bu
a spiritual union with my husband would be
to me than all besides. But, alas! I hear li
my house but disputations about religious opi
My duty is, on those occasions, to pray for M
and his people. I have sometimes erred in
cating myself. My grace, my opinions, my
tice, and even my understanding, are all call
question; all disputed. Well: "It is the
let him do what seemeth him good: I will be
indignation of the Lord, because I have s
against him."

"April 1. My dear husband reproache
with want of affection; he distresses himself
things that have no existence. I have endeav
to trace the cause. I do, through infirmity,
many little attentions: but his prejudice a
the Methodists is unconquerable; and I h

" July 14. My journal has been neglected. The dangerous state of my husband's health has excited much anxiety in my mind. His residence in the country has failed of effect. Often have I wept and pleaded with God on his account, and on account of his flock."

[Mr. Wren died August the 4th; but the account of his death is cut out of the journal: yet she repeatedly adds, that the Lord had afforded her satisfaction of his soul being saved, in answer to prayer. In her journal, we find frequent prayers, that the Lord would bless the account published of his life and death. Her brother also, the Rev. Dr. Mortimer, died about three weeks after Mr. Wren, having enjoyed his preferments but a short time. After this double stroke of Providence, we find Mrs. Wren reverting back to the bands and classes of the Methodists, and walking in the light of God's countenance.]

" Jan. 19, 1785. Praying this morning, that I might be useful, and qualified to do good, many promises were given me to that effect. And when I reviewed the troubles I have endured of late, I was very much encouraged by these words, " Because thou hast kept the words of my patience, I also will keep thee in the hour of temptation," Rev. iii. 10.

" This evening, Mr. Alexander Mather spoke beautifully on purity of heart, defining it under the three ideas, of purity of intention; purity of desire; and purity of affection. He enlarged on the danger of losing our first love, which might be known by the loss of our zeal, and peace, and joy: he insisted, that they who lost these, could not grow in grace till they repented, and did their first works.

" Jan. 28. Mr. Pilmor's sermon was made an abundant blessing to me a few evenings ago. Many promises were brought to my mind, importing, that God had cleansed my heart. I was much

enabled to speak of it in my band. I feel not
in my heart but love to God, and love to
mankind.

"Feb. 21. A sweet persuasion rested upor
this morning, that the Lord had cleansed my h
from sin, and much divine love was shed abroa
my heart: still my cry is, that the Lord w
make me "perfect and entire, lacking nothing

"March 28. To-day we had our quarte
meeting in the forenoon, and love-feast after
ner. My soul was very happy, and wholly g
up to God. A sweet sense rested on my n
that I did, in a measure, enjoy "the full assur
of hope." This has latterly been the case sev
times; and, while in this frame, all earthly ob
have been dispersed before me. I feel a lon
for that holy chastity of spirit, that I may neve
thought, word, or deed, offend my Saviour,
walk in all well-pleasing in his sight."

[St. Paul, after laying down five grand marl
a primitive conversion, adds, "We desire
every one of you do shew the same diligence
the FULL ASSURANCE OF HOPE, unto the end:
ye be not slothful, but followers of them
through faith and patience inherit the promi
And he superadds, that the promise made
Abraham, on leaving Haran, Gen. xii. and
oath confirmed to him when he had offered
Isaac his son, xxii. 16, are the two immut
things, in which it is impossible for God to
and, consequently, the ground of the strong co
lation to a Christian, who has fled for refuge to
hold on the hope set before him: hence we
infer, that Abraham entered into that blessed s
of the full assurance of hope unto the end, v

nest of the Spirit in our hearts," this full assu-
ice cannot imply less, than a salvation from
welling sin: and though it affords strong con-
ation to any highly favoured soul that, like St.
ul, has fought the good fight, 2 Tim. iv. 7, 8,
it is connected with three conditions: negative-
be not slothful; positively, be diligent; and,
tly, be diligent unto the end, as those who,
ough faith and patience, inherit the promises.
After this very pious woman had survived her
ious trials, and made a happy progress in the
of grace, God was providing for her a line of
suitable to her piety, and to her wishes of use-
less in the church. Mr. John Pawson had been
erintendant of the York circuit during her first
rriage: he had known her worth, and how much
gold had been refined in the fire. About the
t of January, this year, he had written to consult
h Mr. Mather, on the propriety of making her
offer of marriage; and Mrs. Mather had named
subject to her, and the communication had
asioned many remarks in her journal of a cau-
is nature, lest she should err a second time.
was not ignorant of his superior worth; both

DOAST.

" The next morning he called ag
his temporal affairs, and still spoke
composed, cool, and rational way. I
to consider of it prior to the ensuin
So we parted, with my consent to cor
" After he was gone, though I wa
prised at the coolness of his address,
calm, and confidence in the Lord, ar
serenity rested on my soul. I felt
perturbation, hesitation, and uncert
had followed me, at every step, in n
riage. The spirit of prayer and inter
upon me most of the day.

" May 8. I felt much of the Lor
my soul was like " the chariots of
The word, all this Sabbath, was spir
me; and I wrestled with the Lord
precious promises in the establishmen
with grace, and in qualifying me for t
his church, which I was called to f
creature seemed as nothing, compar
whom my soul loveth.

" July 1. I was much in prayer, t
stant and uniform sense of the divine
with me. I have latterly prayed to ha
standing, will, affections, and imagin
sanctified; that is, in a greater degre
sent. My confidence, as to the ble
sanctification, was lately put to the
told, that the woman who goes my
spoken disrespectfully of me. For o
seemed as if I felt anger; I answere

the wound was healed, and I felt the Holy Spirit shine on his own work of grace in my soul."

[Mr. Pawson came to York from the conference, and gave her his hand at the altar, on the 14th of August, 1785; and, in a few days after, took her to Edinburgh, where he laboured for two years, spending a part of the time at Glasgow. Here she found herself in that sphere of life for which she seemed formed by nature and grace. She cordially united with her husband, in devoting body and soul, time and talents, yea, and fortune too, wholly to God; and, having no children, they were both the more at leisure for their master's work. Every morning, about seven o'clock, Mr. Pawson came out of his study, read a chapter, sung a hymn, and prayed with his family.

While Mrs. Pawson remained in Scotland, she was largely engaged in a course of reading, and wrote but little in her journal. Her remarks are generally brief; but her stay in the north comprised two of the happiest years of her life.]

" Sept. On arriving at Edinburgh, I was humbled by a sense of my deficiency, and I prayed earnestly, that I might glorify God in the station I was called to fill, and that all my outward conduct might be as becometh the gospel of Christ. Our house is a small one, but God condescends to make it his abode.

" Nov. 1. Having formed a band with Lady Maxwell, and two other pious women, I was much in prayer that it might prosper, and that we might be a blessing to one another. I felt a sweet sense of the assurance of hope spring up in my heart.

" Aug. 26, 1786. To-day I opened my heart, in the fullest manner, in our little band, respecting all my spiritual views: we were all agreed to press after those glorious things to which we are called in Christ Jesus, and not to rest in present attainments.

" On Sunday, Sept. 6, the Lord greatly blessed

class; heaven largely opened on my
was refreshed with love, and peace, a
I have often been grieved and depress
dulness and formality which pervade
professors in Scotland; every one see
less to slumber, ministers not except
cried earnestly to the Lord for Zion t
in this kingdom, and that her glory
forth as a lamp that burneth.

"Leeds, Aug. 31. We arrived
2d of this month. Being much enga
ing and writing, I have neglected my
many months. The Lord has been gr
rying on his work in my soul: the tim
theless, been a constant warfare. Tho
directly say, that I have felt inbred sir
injections have often been so powerful
had enough to do to keep my natural
affections within bounds: on this accou
have often hung down, and the en
failed to augment the discouragement.
shows me that I am called, every mom
and act as in his immediate presence,
after those higher attainments in gra
set before me; such as, the abiding wi
full assurance of hope unto the end

made a pillar in the temple of God, to go out, or be removed, no more for ever."

"I have lately read several comments on the book of Revelation, and made a copious collection of extracts from those authors. We seem to be on the eve of a great enlargement of the Redeemer's kingdom, of the destruction of anti-christ, and of the diffusion of sacred knowledge through all the earth. In reading the Prophets, my soul has likewise been often kindled with the flame of divine love, and enlarged in prayer, for the accomplishment of all the precious promises God has given to his church. The zeal of the Lord of hosts will perform his faithful word.

"Sept. 12. Taking tea with Mrs. Downe,* and a few friends, I greatly admired her method of speaking to a sister who was seeking full salvation: she recommended a continual looking to receive it by faith; and, at the same time, to mortify every propensity, and check every desire, which would obstruct the progress of the work, cherishing also whatever was found to promote a growth in grace: yet she would have people plead nothing that they have done, but only what Christ hath purchased. She liked persons to come into the liberty from a heart-felt sense of the want of it. She by no means approved of loose professors being exhorted to believe, and believe; she thought, the first concern of many should be, to get restored to a justified state, and then to seek the perfect love of God.

"Oct. 3. To-day the spirit of prayer rested upon me for two hours, that I might be useful, and

* This lady was a model of piety. She was daughter of a Turkey merchant in London, and sister of the late Rev. Mr. Furley, Vicar of ———, near St. Austle, who was a friend and correspondent of Mr. Wesley's. Mrs. Downe had been a member of the Methodist society in London. She left a large diary of her experience; but, being written in a peculiar kind of short hand, no person has been found that could read it: hence, no account of her conversion and piety has been given to the church. The disclosure of her worth is reserved for a better world.

fill the place Providence had assigned me, with acceptance. My privileges are great, and I feel myself but as a little child, compared with those wise and holy women with whom I have the happiness to converse.

"Nov. 4. At my band, Mrs. Downe was exceedingly profitable to me. She spoke well of our pilgrimage, and of our exercises by the way, and illustrated what she said, by some remarks of Mr. Fletcher's, in his sermon on Gen. xii. "Now, the Lord had said unto Abraham, get thee out of thy country," &c. He observed, that while we walked by faith, we moved forward towards heaven, as Abraham to the promised land; that God will accomplish his promise to us as to the Patriarch, " I will guide thee continually; yes, in every step we take, whether temporal or spiritual, he will shine upon our path. And as Abraham went out, not knowing whither he went, so should we obey, and follow the light of God's word and grace; for the great mean of a growth in grace is, to keep the heart fixed on God alone, and not suffer it to dwell on any other object longer than duty requires." In this meeting, I felt a powerful sense of the Lord's presence, which was followed by a power to devote my body and soul, my life and health, my husband and friends, wholly to the Lord. I long for all my habits in private, and all my conversation in public, to be wholly under the influence of the Spirit. The Lord is often as a place of broad rivers to my soul.

"May 4, 1788. Miss Ritchie has been in Leeds for some days: I find her conversation, as I have ever done, full of life, and seasoned with salt. Our Saviour bids us to gather up the fragments, that nothing be lost; hence, after being in company with friends who so much surpass me in wisdom and grace, I have often entered in my journal the more striking remarks of conversation, because it is food for my soul, when I read it at a future and habitual walk with God; and this must extend, not only to our words and actions, but also to our thoughts, and to whatever else has the least tendency to damp the vigour of the mind. There were, she observed, a number of things, best known to ourselves, which, by renouncing, would lead us to a more enlarged and immediate intercourse with God; for every degree of self-denial was the acquisition of a degree of grace. By looking unto Jesus, strength would be imparted for the duty; and by the constant exercise of this virtue, one hardly knows the degree of sanctification to which we may attain.

"I was not less edified by her method of leading the class. She recommended us to come to the Lord with our present power, which would increase by exercise. Of one who was thirsting for full redemption she inquired, whether the sister was willing to give up all for Christ? On being answered in the affirmative, she advised her to be constantly offering up her all in sacrifice, waiting for the Lord to accept the oblation of her heart, by coming in the power of his Spirit, to cleanse, and fill it with love. Another, who complained of the obstinacy of her will, and the warmth of her tempers, she advised to mortify every temper contrary to love, looking, at the same time, every moment for a full deliverance, as we must never rest in present attainments. A backslider, who was present, she advised to get properly sensible of her loss, and then not to be discouraged from coming immediately to God with a contrite heart. She advised me, a hurry of my natural spirits being always an impediment of my progress, to be still, and to know God. On Mrs. Baines' complaining, that whenever she had grieved the Spirit of God, she sunk into discouragement, and con-

cluded; that she must go through a long
sorrow before she could find comfort
rejoined, that much of those fears aro[se]
work of the law, and that, on feeling a
of having grieved the Holy Spirit, in ar[e]
are called immediately to look to God f[or]
we must not allow the mirror to rem[ain]
but continually endeavour to behold t[he]
glory of the Lord, and it will become b[y]
our faith increases." [It is to be regre[tted]
from the brevity of Mrs. Pawson's journ[al]
not give the reader a fair specimen of
method of meeting a class.]

"Dec. 4. The last week has been
prayer and intercession with my soul, fo[r]
persons in the church. I have often be[en on my]
knees for two hours, praying for the
others in trouble. I feel grateful to th[e]
many mercies. My brother, in a late vis[it,]
received me very kindly.

"Dec. 26. On Friday last my broth[er]
was laid on my mind, and I wrestled [with the]
Lord an hour and a half, that he wou[ld overcome]
the prejudices they have imbibed agains[t me;]
and to-day I received a letter from m[y sister, to]
inform me, that my brother was ver[y ill, and]
attended by two physicians. I hasted [to him,]
and found him sensible. He admitted
him for two minutes: I embraced the m[an, and]
speak to him wholly of his salvation: [the]
nurse hurried me away, alleging, that [he wished]
to sleep. I retired, and wrestled with th[e Lord to]
spare him, till his soul exhibited some [marks of]
regeneration; and the Lord wonderful[ly poured]
upon me a spirit of prayer on his a[ccount. I]
awoke the next morning at one o'clock [and felt]
the same spirit of prayer to rest upon [me on his]
account. Lady Anderson and the nurs[e in-]
formed me, that he was much in prayer, [that on Christ]
he placed his hope, and his only ho[pe.]

Saviour. From these circumstances, and from the liberty I found for him in prayer, I have hopes of his salvation. He settled his affairs three days before his death; but, on adding a codicil to his will, in favour of his grandson, he said, I have forgotten my sister; put her down a legacy. He died Dec. —, aged sixty, leaving three children.

"July 13. I have, this evening, enjoyed an abundant spirit of gratitude for the mercies I received of the Lord: health, happiness, yea, and peace amid my transient trials; and all these blessings seem crowned with the best of husbands; a man of regular piety; and no one surpasses him in the uprightness of his intentions: truly my heart overflows with a sense of the goodness and love of God. O! it is best, far the best, for my soul to look immediately to Jesus, and not to be discouraged by any momentary wanderings of the mind. A fresh act of faith always brings fresh comfort and strength. In this way I would forget the things behind, and reach forth to the things before, and always realize a sense of the presence of God.

"Aug. 24. We arrived at Birstal about a week ago. After living more than fifty years in large towns, I here found myself in a secluded house, and among strangers. The separation from so many valuable friends in Leeds, and the idea of a country life for the future, seemed to give the enemy an advantage to tempt me; but, on looking to the Lord, I found strength to give up my will to his will. We had been invited to Hull; but Mr. Wesley, who lodged with us during the conference, thought it best to station my husband here, that he might endeavour to compose some religious disputes which had broken out in this society. Hence I saw it my duty to improve every thing designed for good, and willingly to take up every cross: and, as to the loss of my Christian friends, I believe the Lord himself is able to supply the

cies of the past year: they are great and man
have a husband, to whom I feel an increa
affection; not one jarring string exists to occ
discord in our happiness; but, on the contrar
increase of mutual affection. Another sour
gratitude is, the kindness of so many val
friends in Leeds; and the many marks of affe
and esteem which they conferred upon me.
health, my temporal mercies, yea, mercies v
I cannot count, all call upon me to devot
future life to God, which I hope to do wi
reserve.

"Jan. 1, 1790. I desire to begin afresh, i
spiritual progress, and to be particularly gua
against every thing that has been a hinderan
me in the preceding year. I have had many
flicts of late, and have often been but just s
now, in the strength of God, I will arise, and
the kingdom of heaven by a holy violence. I
discovered several things of late, in which I
been led by my own spirit, and not by the
of the Lord. This humbles me at the thro
grace, and makes me desirous to have my
heart subdued, and my will swallowed up i
will of God.

"Jan. 22. A very solemn sense of divine t
rested on my mind all the day. The Lord
me light into many of Satan's devices, with
I have lately been exercised. It is quite wro
judge of our state according to the accusatic
the enemy, though even his suggestions were
for he draws discouraging inferences from
defects, and would drive us to seek salvati
the works of the law. He always endeavou

...od, to keep my eye constantly fixed on the hope ... before me, looking for the mercy of our Lord ...sus Christ, unto eternal life.

"Feb. 3. I have been happy, as usual, in my ...ul, lively in the class, and I see some little fruit ... my labours. My husband and I, this morning, ...oked over our temporal affairs. How thankful ...ould we be, that we have enough, and to spare. ...he language of my heart is, not to lay up treasure ... earth. I feel desirous to give more largely to ...e cause of God, and to the poor; for it is more ...essed to give than to receive.

"Feb. 15. A spirit of wrestling and supplica-...on was given me, in regard to the disputes with ...r. Atlay at Dewsbury. A railing spirit seems to ...edominate, which must lead to painful issues, ...th as to the piety, and the usefulness of the par-...s. The Lord, however, sweetly draws me to ...ok to him, and gives me the spirit of prayer for ... husband, in all these difficulties. My heart ...elts with love and affection for him, when I see ...m tried; and a thousand instances of his kindness ... me are brought to my recollection, to enlarge my ...art in prayer for him: however, the Lord shews ...e, that we must live daily in the spirit of sacrifice, ...d in all submission to his holy will. Amid all ...ese difficulties, my soul is broken down at the ...ord's feet, and weaned, in some sort, from all ...eated good.

"May 14. I am just returned from Leeds, ...here Mr. Wesley has been for some days. My ...eart glowed with love on meeting my dear friends ... the Lord, and I found them lively and affec-...onate as usual. The precious opportunities I ...njoyed among them at tea, and in the classes, and ...ands, were as the dew of Hermon to my soul.

our understanding given up, that the po[
Christ may rest upon us. Miss Ritchie en
on the hint dropped by Mr. Blair, concerni
only our understanding, but all our sens[
affections given up to Christ. She observe[
faith, in some sort, was a new sense, and an[
to our natural senses. The soul has an e[
ear, and a taste: and that the grand point
get all these senses hallowed and strengt[
then every other Christian temper would [
tionably grow and increase.

"But I cannot repeat all the good things]
from Mrs. Crosby, Mrs. Downe, and others.
only add, that those little parties, and class[
bands, are the beginning of the heavenly so[
this lower world. The preaching, likewis[
profitable to my soul." Mr. Mather delive[
excellent sermon on faith, hope, and char[
observed, that charity was greater than th[
two graces, because it made us resemble Go[

"July 11. Of late, I have been harass[
the enemy. Sometimes I have rejoiced
assurance of hope; and, at other times, Sa[
endeavoured to rob me of it, and to beclo[
understanding, hurry my spirits, and repro[
for every misplaced word, with the flashes
law. This morning, I was much blessed
Mr. Entwisle's sermon. My communion w[
was enlarged, and a spiritual view of the as[
of hope, opened to my soul."

"August 18. I have been once more, w[
husband was absent at the Conference, to
friends in Leeds, Thorner, and York.

this visit, I left the Lord with me; but had some reason to be ashamed for not glorifying him more among the different families I visited. I have to lament also that I did not find the classes so lively as I expected: yet I found power to breathe out my soul in prayer for a revival of religion among them.

"Nov. 18. Mr. Mather preached at Birstal this evening, and took a bed with us. His text was, 2 John, ver. 8: 'Look to yourselves, that ye lose not the things that we have wrought, but that we receive a full reward.' Many, he observed, revolted at the word *reward*, being biassed by a system. He fully allowed, that all grace came from God; nevertheless, we were called to improve our talent, and to work out our own salvation. Aided by the power and grace of the promises, we are enjoined to cleanse ourselves from all defilement of the flesh and spirit. Consequently, by our not working with the grace, we are in danger of losing the reward of holiness. He proceeded, in the same line, 'unto the full assurance of hope unto the end.' While pursuing the path of obedience, the blessings in the text, called 'a full reward,' are conferred upon us. At the same time, he cautiously added, that we can have no claim to merit, all being purchased by the Redeemer's blood. He then urged us to look for a present and a future reward, as Heb. xii. 2: 'for eye hath not seen, ear hath not heard, neither have entered into the heart of man, the things God hath prepared for them that love him,' 1 Cor. ii. 9.

"Feb. 25. This evening, I was nearly two hours on my knees, pleading with the Lord for the full assurance of hope, and that the Lord would undertake for me in all my conflicts with the enemy. Sometimes I have clear views of the blessing I am seeking; and sometimes all has appeared to me dark, and Satan disputing with me every inch of ground. The Lord has long shown me the want centre.

" March 5. . We have just received the printed letter of Mr. Wesley's death, after a few days' illness, on the second of this month. A prince —a great man, is fallen in our Israel. It is a great stroke to the church;—but Zion has still her God. The pillars fall, and the house stands. The Lord, who called him to this work, has given him a life of almost uninterrupted health for nearly eighty-eight years. And the Lord has spared him till the foundation of Methodism is adequately laid. There are now many pious and able ministers to carry on the work, that this revival of religion may spread to the uttermost parts of the earth. I believe it will be a time of fervent prayer for the preachers and the whole connexion.

" March 20. My husband preached Mr. Wesley's funeral sermon to-day, from Heb. xiii. 7, and I think I never heard him speak with more unction and power. I have been much stirred up also by hearing Mr. Percival this year. His word is generally attended with good to my soul.

" July 8. I have been, of late, much engaged with God for my husband, that he may, at the approaching Conference, be endowed with meekness, patience, and fortitude, to contend for whatever is right in the connexion, that we may still spend our lives, labours, and fortune, in the Lord's work. I would willingly make a free-will of all at the feet of Jesus.

" Amidst all, I still keep the prize in view, which I have long been pursuing; and I do feel, that my soul prospers only in proportion as I keep it in view.

" July 23, to August 2. On coming to Leeds,

I had some very gracious seasons at the band, and in other opportunities, with my friends. Mrs. Downe spoke her experience first among the sisters, and was very encouraging to others. Miss Lucas spoke in a very profitable manner, concerning the necessity of living in the spirit of every office and duty to which we were called. I have felt my soul much revived among them, and have been enabled to rejoice in hope of receiving the blessing for which I have been long looking. I have received a very consoling letter from my husband, of the peace and union of the Conference. Surely this is of God, for the preachers were left as children without a father.

"Aug. 31. We have been at Halifax a week. Our house, under the chapel, seems but gloomy; and I was at first discouraged, in seeing no openings to be useful. However, I have found here, as at Leeds, women to whom I feel united; and hope that we shall be useful to one another. A class has been given me to lead, and I have opportunities of meeting a few friends, who are athirst for a full salvation.

"Oct. 23. I have been much edified by reading once more the account of Mr. Fletcher's death. Mrs. F. asked him, whether there was any thing, in particular, he would recommend to her? His reply comforted me much, 'The Lord will open the way before you.' The expression came with power, and I was much engaged with God that it might be the case.

"Jan. 1, 1792. On reading over my journal for the last year, I see that the enemy has gained many advantages over me. *First*, my will has not been wholly subdued to the will of God. *Secondly*, I have failed in many points of duty towards Esther, my old and faithful servant. *Thirdly*, I have not been sufficiently aware of our Saviour's caution concerning entering into temptation. *Fourthly*, I have not prayed for the tempted, and the fallen, failed in praying for those heights and depths of grace which I see before me; but I feel resolved to cast myself at the Lord's feet, as the most unprofitable of his followers, and to set out anew for that better country to which Abraham aspired.

"Feb. 5. My mind has been more free than usual from temptations. I have delighted in reading the holy Scripture. A passage in the Revelation was made very useful to me; and I believe the Lord is deepening his work in my soul, purifying my affections, and loosening my heart from the earth.

"May 10. My journal has been neglected. I regret the omission, as the reading of it is often profitable to my soul. Mr. Entwisle was married to our niece on the second of this month, and with our fervent prayers for their mutual happiness.

"To-day my husband gave the Sacrament in his own house; a custom he has ever continued since we went into Scotland. But, if giving the Sacrament in our chapels will occasion any division, I know he will prefer the union of the body, and administer it no where in public. I have found those ordinances very refreshing to my soul. Some of my late exercises seem to have strengthened my faith; and I feel a sweet peace in giving up my own will.

"Dec. 23. My old friend, Miss Rhodes, of Leeds, is now on a visit at Mr. Richard Emmet's. Her conversation has been as salt to my soul. I find much union of spirit with her. Our conversation was without reserve. She made free to tell me, that she observed in me a desire to please, which would produce a degree of bondage. I was grateful for the hint, as the desire of my soul has been to be free from all inordinate attachment to persons, or places, or objects. She mentioned Mrs. Fletcher, as having so strong an attachment to her husband, that it was not, till three years after his death, that she could completely rise above it. This conversation induced me to pray for an hour, that I might rise above every thing which might have an undue ascendancy over my heart.

"Jan. 1, 1793. After reading over my journal, I sit down to make a calm review of the past year. 1. My leading efforts have been to purify my affections from the earth. In this view, I sigh for a farther liberty. 2. I have been often favoured with the spirit of prayer for my husband, that the Lord would support him in all the cares of the ministry, and give him wisdom. when preachers write to him for advice. 3. Our temporal property having increased in the funds, I feel a desire to dispose of it as the Lord shall please. I desire no more of worldly riches, than what I shall improve to the glory of God. 4. I feel no thirsting after spiritual honour. 5. I see that the Lord has not taken me to the mount to be filled with unutterable joy; but he has led me in a humble path, and through many conflicts, to be delivered from all undue attachment to every thing on earth. Yet, in all my weaknesses and conflicts, I have never once disputed my having been delivered from indwelling sin. On the whole, this has been a year of many trials, and of many blessings to my soul. The Lord has taught my hands to war, and my fingers to fight. My husband's sermons have often been very refreshing and encouraging.

"April 13. The following extract of Miss Ritchie's letter to Miss Rhodes, has struck me as worthy a transcription into my journal: 'Never did I see more need than lately of that exhortation, Grieve not the Spirit. A thousand little inattentions the divine teachings, will become more and more sensible of the guiding eye, the leading hand, the directing voice, which say to those who are wishful not to rest in any thing short of it, The anointing which ye have received of him abideth in you; and ye need not that any man teach you, but as the same anointing teacheth you of all things, and is truth, and is no lie, and even as it hath taught you that ye shall abide in him, 1 John ii. 27. [This is St. John's caveat against false teachers.] And truly, I see no other way of profiting by all I meet with, whether means, or friends, or providences, or whatever else, but to get under the Spirit's influence.'

"Reading the above passage was made a blessing to my soul. The Spirit of grace and supplication rested upon me, that I might be governed by his teaching, and always act under his influences.

"July. Being at Leeds, during the Conference, the hurry of the time deprives me of enjoying that spiritual intercourse with my friends to which I have been accustomed. My husband is elected president, (being the third after Mr. Wesley's death;) and this honour is so far from lifting me up, that I feel it humbles me at the Lord's feet. I poured out my soul for him, that he might be directed in the knotty points of discipline which now agitate the connexion. Our appointment is this year for Liverpool, with Mr. (now Dr.) Adam Clarke.

"Oct. Since I came to this town, I have not lived so near to God as I did at Halifax. I have been hurried with visiting, and exercised with many domestic concerns. I am appointed to lead a class, and have formed a band. The preaching of brother Clarke and my husband, is very profitable to my soul. Brother Clarke is, in my estination, an extraordinary preacher; and his learning confers great lustre on his talents: he makes it subservient to grace: his discourses are highly evangelical: he never loses sight of Christ. In regard of pardon and holiness, he offers a present salvation. His address is lively, animated, and very encouraging to the seekers of salvation. To the unawakened, it may indeed be said, that he obeys that precept, 'Cry aloud; spare not; lift up thy voice like a trumpet,' &c. His words flow spontaneously from the heart; his views enlarge as he proceeds; and he brings to the mind a torrent of things new and old. While he is preaching, one can seldom cast an eye on the audience, without perceiving a melting unction resting upon them. His 'speech distils as the dew, and as the small rain upon the tender herb.' He generally preaches from some part of the lesson for the day; and, on the Sabbath morning, from the gospel for the day: this method confers an abundant variety in his ministry.

"May 30, 1794. For six years past I have had a daily cross, which I have borne in much silence, in obedience to my husband, and to God. Mr. Pawson, with the most humane of motives, has taken under his patronage a desolate niece: we have put her to school, and discharged our duty to her as a daughter; yet, from the peculiar obstinacy of her temper, I have discharged the duty as a cross, not as a delight. I have looked upon her living with us, as an exercise to my faith and patience, and, on that account, I have borne it as from the Lord. This little task has been alleviated by the kindness of the best of husbands.

"July 3, 1795. My mind has been mostly in a good frame since we came to Liverpool; and I have been led to pray for several persons who have thought lightly of me, that every spiritual blessing may be poured upon them. I have likewise wrestled much with God for the whole connexion, lest

it should be torn to pieces about points of disc
pline—points which will subside of themselves,
the parties will have a little forbearance with on
another.

"London, Aug. I feel much of the spirit (
prayer given me, that the Lord would unite th
hearts of the preachers and the trustees, that a
disputes may be amicably adjusted, and the powei
ful spirit of intercession is mostly to be regarded a
a pledge that God will give an answer of peace.

"Oct. Mr. Thompson, of Hull, Mr. Mathei
and my husband, thank God, have succeeded i
procuring peace. We have a fine prospect i
regard to hearers. A class here also is assigne
me to meet. I find the people exceedingly kin
and affectionate.

"Jan. 1, 1796. Since we have been in Londor
I have, in general, walked in the light of God
countenance, and felt as much of the spirit (
prayer as formerly, for the church and for indivi
duals. The ministry of my husband is, in parti
cular, made a blessing to me; and the ministry (
Mr. Griffith is very edifying and pleasing. I ar
still following after the full assurance of hope unt
the end; but I see that I have not a single though
to purchase it; therefore I must plead for it solel
on the ground of what Jesus Christ has suffered fc
me. Sometimes I have felt great poverty of spiri
which is ever followed by a gracious frame, and
have been enabled to present it as a sacrifice to th
Lord.

"Our select band was remarkably edifying th
last evening. Brother R. was encouraging to th
seekers of a full salvation. He particularly urge
them, in whatever state they might be, to give u
no part of their attainments, because it was not th
whole. Brother George Whitefield, wishful to ei
courage one who was dejected, reminded him (
Samson, who still made efforts after his locks wei
shorn; and of a man with the withered hand, who

Jesus commanded to stretch it forth. What a privilege to hear persons, of so much wisdom and experience, speak of the work of grace!

"April 11. To-day I visited a member of our society, who has been very much conformed to the world. She was convinced, a few days ago, of her error, under a sermon of my husband's. I spoke plainly with her on the subject of dress. How difficult it is to persuade some professors to take the plainest, and, eventually, the easiest road to heaven!

"July. I have lately passed through many trials, it being the divine pleasure that I should bear my frequent cross. I must drink of my Lord and Master's cup. He tasted of the bitter potion on the cross; and left what remained for others to drink: but, amidst the whole, I drink also of the cup of salvation. On Sunday last, while brother W. Griffith preached, my soul was as a watered garden. His text was, Isa. ii. 5, 'O house of Israel, come ye, and let us walk in the light of the Lord.' I have not had so refreshing a season for several years.

"The Conference is just at hand, and the preachers are beginning to come. My heart is enlarged for the prosperity of Zion. It is a day of trouble to the connexion. Alexander Kilham has agitated the minds of the Methodists, by the circulation of many anonymous printed letters, &c. His whole attack seems levelled at the old preachers. He seems to wish the Methodists to adopt, as far as possible, the laws of the French National Assembly. But to insinuate that my husband, and other venerable men, have defrauded the connexion, after devoting our lives and fortune to the cause, is cruel in the extreme. Well, the church has often had to endure the contradiction, and the sneers of restless men. The preachers have all been united in his expulsion; and, if he do not retract his slanders, God will inflict upon him a heavier

have just learned, that several of the preac
have been remarkably 'useful to the families w
they lodged. Several persons have been se
liberty under their prayers. They are now ;
as harvest-men to their Master's work.
"Dec. 17. I have found much edificatio
reading one of Mr. Fletcher's letters; it has
me to an increase of faith; and I do feel a p
to give my whole heart to God. My prayer i

'Take my body, spirit, soul,
Only thou possess the whole."

"I feel the spirit of prayer also to rest upor
for the church, that the Lord would bless
preachers in this circuit, and take the affairs o
whole connexion into his own hands. Somet
I have prayed for the whole day, with the al
ance of short intervals of repose. It is a dark
cloudy day for Methodism. May it emerge w
divine radiance, and illuminate the world.

"June 6, 1797. I have neglected my jou
having been much employed in transcribing
able letters for the Methodist Magazine; but I
enjoyed much nearness to God, and the guid
of his Holy Spirit. This evening, at the {
band, I was edified by the remark of a friend
cerning the exercise of faith. 'While we
looking,' he said, 'for the fulfilment of any
mise, and while our eye is constantly fixe
Jesus, we always receive something; and we sl
never be discouraged because we do not receiv
whole of what is promised: we should be tha
for the smallest measure of grace, and hold fa:
beginning of our confidence to the end.'
was exceedingly pertinent to my case. I have
but slowly reaching forth, and pressing towar
mark, that I might attain the full assurance of

unto the end. I see, in all my conflicts, that I must not parley with the enemy; but guard the grace which God has planted in my heart. All our armour is defensive, except the sword; hence, I see my call to watch, and not to suffer Satan to gan advantages over me, by the daily incidents of life.

"Dec. 19. This day our beloved Sovereign went in procession to St. Paul's, to return thanks to Almighty God for his recovery. I had the offer of two stands to see the procession; but chose rather to spend the time in grateful solitude. The Methodists, throughout England and Ireland, had held a special, but unostentatious, day of fasting and prayer for his recovery, just before the happy event.

"I have lately heard an excellent sermon, from the Rev. Mr. Eyres, of Hommerton: he preached in the City-Road chapel. The object of his sermon was, to promote a friendly union between the Methodists and the Dissenters. There was an uncommon degree of unction attendant on his word. I wept much, and felt my affections expanded to all the children of God. The whole congregation was affected.

'Happy day of union sweet;
  Lord, when shall it appear!
When shall all thy people meet,
  In amity sincere!
Tear each other's flesh no more,
  But kindly think and speak the same;
All express the meek'ning power,
  And spirit, of the Lamb.'

WESLEY.

"Jan. 1, 1798. My soul, for some time past, has been in the usual way. On some occasions, the spirit of prayer has been given me for the church, and I have wrestled much with God for the pros-

perity of Zion, and could not desist till my hu:
has raised me from my knees.

"Oct. 3. My journal has been neglected
months, partly by the hurry of the Conference
partly by preparing the house for Mr. M:
My husband seems quite as happy since our r
val to Spitalfields, as at the New Chapel, whe
had the preachers to converse with; and we
found the people equally kind to us; and it
satisfaction to me, that my class is incre:
besides, my soul has prospered since we
hither. I have been enabled to maintain a
stant intercourse with God, and a daily wa
upon him for the full assurance of hope.

"Aug. 1799. By the Bristol conference,
were, a second time, appointed for Leeds. I
spent four happy years in London; and espe
the last year, while we resided at Spitalfields.
friends were remarkably affectionate to me;
love begets love. I should have thought n
happy to have ended my days in London; bi
must ever live prepared to embrace the wi
Providence.

"No sooner have I returned from Yor
Leeds, than I find myself at home. The kin
of my friends and relatives has humbled me m
and my intimacy and union of spirit seer
increase with Mrs. Crosby, sister Tripp,
Rhodes, and others. Miss Rhodes being of
with me, I feel a particular union with her, fou
on a persuasion that we are mutually benefici
each other.

"Dec. 23. I took tea at Miss Maud's, w
select party of Christian friends. Among th
cellent subject of the conversation, Mrs. C
gave me a profitable hint for meeting cl:
She did not always approve of exhorting pe
to believe, and believe; but rather to find ou
hinderances of their faith. They should the

exhorted to lay those hinderances all aside, and pray the Holy Spirit so to shine on their mind, that they may see the little foxes which spoil the vine. She thought I dwelt too much on the best things, having, while in London, made them the daily subjects of conversation. Miss R. agreed, that the mind of Christ consisted in possessing the lovely tempers of our living Head; and, also, in feeling sorrow for many in the church of God, and in weeping for mankind. She then enlarged on embracing the whole will of God in all his dispensations; and the conversations of these friends were not only edifying, but, indeed, a mirror to my heart. I was comforted, because I often felt that spirit which not only weeps, but wrestles, for mankind.

"On being asked, what was the best method for a soul to take, which had lost the earnest, either of justification, or of sanctification; she replied, that the soul, in this case, was to be compared to the body. When the latter is unhealthy, we avoid whatever tends to keep it so; and, on the other hand, we use every endeavour to remove its indisposition. Thus the soul, whenever its fervent desires after God are abated, should lay aside whatever obstructs a return of the consolations of the Holy Spirit; such as, the indulgence of earthly comforts, and use the means of grace with more fervour; thereby it would acquire a spiritual appetite; and God would satisfy its hunger and thirst after righteousness.

"Leeds, Jan. 1, 1800. This morning was much blessed to my soul, under a sermon on Zechariah

increase in spiritual discernment to
power to do the will of God.

"Jan. 31. To-day I found muc
meeting Miss Tripp's class; and in
was much edified by the conversation
friends. Miss R. observed, that wh
given, we must practise self-denial,
cross, and give up our own will, to
light. Recommending some in the
make further sacrifices, she said, that
us to give up whatever was a hinde
growth in grace; and if we gave
would presently shew us more that m
up.

"Feb. 2. A friend repeated in
observation of the Rev. Mr. Cecil's,
judge of people's grace by their frui
always consider what was their na
before conversion; whether it was
and impetuous, as St. Paul's: then gr
itself in zeal, tempered with knowledge
jecting their activity to the wisdom
God. Also, a temper naturally mild,
ought not to be the standard of a

disposition. This remark referred me to my own disposition, which was active, volatile, resolute, ever wishful to be employed, and persevering in its pursuits; but, suffering myself to be drawn after too great a variety of objects, I excel in none. To avoid all confusion in the duties of life, I have often wished to follow Mr. Wesley's example. He considered in a morning what he was called to do; then, unless God ordered otherwise, he endeavoured to do one thing at once, to avoid hurry.

"March 12. This being the Fast-day, I improved the morning in prayer, that God would pardon all my sins of omission, and of commission. I was led out likewise to pray, that he would pardon the sins of all our preachers and people, and of the nation at large." [Here God seems to have led this pious woman to prayer, before the sore trial which came on her and her husband, respecting the volume of seventeen sermons he had printed, as a legacy to the poor, to be given away after his death. Some strictures on the clergy, who do not preach the evangelical doctrines, shamefully distorted, occasioned a severe trial to both their minds; and several friends, who ought to have supported and comforted them, augmented their affliction.]

"Sept. 6. My journal has been long neglected, which I always regret, because it is profitable to review the dealings of God with my soul.

"While my husband has been at the London conference, I have spent a fortnight in York, at Mr. Grey's, and felt great union of spirit with my old friends, many of whom are joined with Mr. R. Several remarks in reading have struck me very forcibly. "If a temptation," says Gurnal, "follow us for any length of time, it is a mark that we have not faithfully resisted the first attacks of the enemy; and that we have partially admitted his

my soul. I saw my weakness and
cried that every Agag might be de[s]
every Isaac sacrificed to the Divine pl[e]

"Nov. 23. The Lord has visited
presence and love; especially for th[e]
weeks, in which I have been much
prayer, that the Lord would take aw[ay]
foxes that spoil my vine, whether the[y]
nature, education, or habit. Satan,
vantage of the weakness of my nerves,
much in those muddy waters, and pr[e]
coming boldly to the throne of grace.
now say, the Lord hath heard my pra[y]
felt much of his love shed abroad in m[y]
been much refreshed in the public mea[ns]
I have been favoured also with much e[ase]
when called to exercise in prayer.

"Birstal, Aug. 28, 1801. Our lot i[s]
in this place. My husband and I 1[ook?]
through deep waters; friend and love[r]
aloof! What an encomium on the dis[ciples]
our Saviour said, These are they tha[t con]tinued with me in my temptations! Bu[t]
throw a mantle of love on the whole. [Mr?]
and I have both been on the borders o[f]
by grief and affliction. The Conferenc[e]
have, in some degree, healed his wou[nd]
by electing him president a second time

"In Birstal, I enjoy a happy retrea[t]
gathering a class, which promises to i[n]
cannot but record my gratitude to Mrs.
Walker, for her kindness to me in man[y]

"There are two habitual defects in my constitution, which have obstructed the blessing I have long been pursuing. The first is, a natural precipitancy of spirit, which has often led me to speak and act dissonant to the will of God. The other defect is, an undue degree of curiosity; and though it may not have hurried me to hurt my conscience in speaking against any one, yet I have been defective in courage to stop the tongue of slander. Now, in waiting for the salvation of God, these things must be laid aside, that we may so hunger and thirst after righteousness as to be filled. The Lord, however, seems sitting upon my heart, as a refining fire, and with the spirit of judgment. I hope he will consume all my defects by his love. I desire that my whole will may be swallowed up in the will of God.

"Dec. 12. During the last fortnight, the Lord has been carrying on his work in my soul, and purifying my affections from those cares and weights which have impeded my progress. During my great and sore trials the last year, the evidence of sanctification has been beclouded, and, for a while, I lost ground. The fight was long and tedious. My natural will and affections were not sufficiently fire. My husband, at the same instant, was crossing the room to the parlour. Impelled by a Divine impulse, I followed him to see if all was well; but scarcely had I reached the door, ere the arch of the chimney, a huge stone of half a ton weight, suddenly fell, followed by the bricks. To all appearance, I must have been buried under the rubbish, had not the care of heaven called me away. May all my added life be devoted to him, who has numbered the hairs of my head.

"My preservation, on this occasion, has induced me afresh to review the mercies of former years, and to see what my defects have been, and what the Lord has brought me through. For twelve years after my being awakened, I attended the church, and the Methodists: I was satisfied of my call to join the Methodists; but a too predominant fear kept me back. Whenever I named it to my mother, it made her ill. After giving up my connexion with Mr. Wren, I was satisfied it was the will of God that I should not renew it; and, in this, the religious friends I consulted were unanimous; yet, through the same fear, I yielded to marry him, notwithstanding the delicate state of his health, lest my retraction should occasion his death: yet it was my sufferings, on that occasion, which chiefly endeared me to my present husband. After Mr. Wren's death, giving myself wholly up to the Lord, I received purity of heart, Jan, 28, 1785, and, in some measure, have held it fast. Yet this passion of fear still pursued me. During the many years that M. J. lived with us, (and, as we had no children, it was the best of deeds in my husband to take care of her,) I was still harassed with the same nervous fear. Once I reproved her, and she threatened to make away with herself, so I durst not reprove again. I was a mother to her, in obedience to God and my husband; and it was a daily cross to live with a person, whose peculiar tempers finally closed in melancholy. The same timidity follows me in regard to the members of my class. When any of them act wrong, I fear to be too severe, lest I should drive them from God. This is my thorn in the flesh. The Lord will not take it away: but his grace being sufficient for me, my call is to fight against it to the end. After I received sanctification, Mrs. Mather advised me to look on every thing as a temptation, which tended to doubt, discouragement, and fear. I see I have erred in not habitually adopting her advice. I feel nothing contrary to love towards any creature, how much soever I may have been tried by different persons; nevertheless, I might have lived more to the glory of God; and I have failed in the purification of my natural will, and my human affections.

"July to August. I have spent some time at Leeds, with Mrs. Dickinson, Miss Lucas, and several other families, to whom my affections are united. We have spent a good year at Birstal. The Lord has owned the ministry of Mr. Pipe and my husband. Many sinners have been awakened, and added to the society. Mr. Pipe is blessed with fine natural powers, and he has been made very useful to me by his preaching. I have seen fruit in my class, it having increased to twenty-three members.

"Bristol, Sept. 25, 1803. It is now five weeks since our arrival in this city. I cannot describe the affection with which my husband has been received by the principal families; and the poor are not less cordial and affectionate. A preacher here is very differently circumstanced from one at Birstal; every thing here among the families, has an appearance of affluence, in some sort, surpassing London. What need, then, to watch? to tremble? to live by rule? always endeavouring to be useful? Surely men deeply engaged in business, have need of something spiritual, when they invite a preacher to their house: they hear enough of the world at other times.

"Dec. 31. With regard to my soul, the preceding year, it has prospered, but not equally to my privileges. I have not improved my dispensation as I ought; may I be more faithful the year which is to come!

"May 15, 1804. My journal has been neglected, owing to the affliction of my servant Esther, and the difficulty of improving time in Bristol. The Lord still continues to enlighten my mind, as to the impediments of my progress. I have erred by a precipitant spirit; and a wish to attain the top of the ladder, without ascending the steps: so I have often had to go back again. Lord, to whom shall I go but unto thee; for thou hast the words of eternal life. I have, however, the consolation to see that my class has increased to thirty-one members.

"Oct. 29. I have just received a letter, apprising me of the death of that valuable woman, Mrs. Crosby, of Leeds. She has been to me a friend, dear as my own soul; and that from my first setting out in religion. Her memory will be dear to me for ever: though dead she seems still talking to me, and a number of her sayings crowd on my remembrance. I hope never to be satisfied, till the truths she used to enforce, be fully written on my heart. Few excelled her in Christian simplicity. Mrs. Mortimer used to say, that she could descend to the capacity of a child, and then rise again to expatiate on the deep things of God, with those that had attained the highest state of grace. But, in point of sympathy, she surpassed all I ever knew. She could so enter into the feelings and concerns of others, as to fulfil the precept, ' Bear ye one another's burdens, and so fulfil the law of Christ.' O, how my soul has been blessed, under her addresses to the throne of grace, when wrestling with God for the flock! She used to begin prayer with the simplicity of a little child, and then rise to the language of a mother in Israel. Thus she prayed with the Spirit, and with the understanding: and the triumph of her death corresponded with the glory of her life. But she also, like me, was assailed with a precipitancy of spirit, and with a zeal which was not always tempered with wisdom. Nevertheless, I can apply to her what I have often heard my husband say of Mr. Wesley, that he had the glory of God in view in all he did. In the early part of her pilgrimage, she stood almost alone for God, and evidenced her love to him by an uniform, warm, and active piety.

"Dec. 9. We have had, this evening, a very precious meeting at the select band. I agree with what I have heard, that faith is an active principle; that it will always bring power, if not much of sensible comfort; that it will always discover, by its fruits, an increase of patience, and resignation, humility, watchfulness, and zeal. Since my sore trials two years ago, I have not enjoyed quite so much of love as usual; yet I never had so great a power over my own spirit as now, nor saw the way so clearly in which I am called to serve and glorify God.

"In reading over my journal, which, indeed, has been the main object of my writing it, I see how often the Lord has poured upon me the Spirit of grace and supplication, and so long, that my husband has sometimes raised me from my knees. But why have not the effects been more lasting? Why has not the glory of grace shone longer on my countenance, and remained in gracious frames on my heart? I clearly perceive, as, indeed, I have long perceived, that my great foible has been, an aptitude to reason with the enemy.

"Wakefield, Aug. 23, 1805. The Conference have appointed us for this circuit. We were invited to York, Wakefield, and London; besides being included in the Manchester and the Liverpool petitions: esteem and honour await the ministry in

ble age. My husband's infirmities require an
sy circuit; hence, I hope our lot is of the Lord.
ir dear friends in Bristol took a most affectionate
ewell of us, not being likely to see us again in
e flesh. I bear on my heart a grateful recollection
Mrs. Castleman, Mrs. Ewer, and many others
that city; and of the favours and blessings
have received among them. On the road, we
re kindly entertained at Thomas Holy's, Esq.
Sheffield, who loves the ministers of Christ
cause of their work.
" Oct. 3. The congregations here are large,
d we indulge the hopes of a revival. Perhaps
is enrages the enemy. One of Mr. Kilham's
lks has just published an anonymous pamphlet,
iefly against my husband. The whole is mis-
ited and untrue. Among other things, he accuses
m with marrying a woman whom he expelled
om the society in York. No; he did not. I re-
ained some months in the Methodist society,
ter my marriage with Mr. Wren; and I inclosed
y ticket to my present husband in a letter, solely
cause Mr. Wren urged it, alleging that my being
Methodist hindered my usefulness to his church.
he design is, to hurt my husband's usefulness in
Wakefield; but it will fail of effect. I wonder
at this party should still fall upon us in old and
ble age; but sometimes the tempest is permitted
rage till the ship reaches port. Well: the will
the Lord be done!
" Dec. 8. My old and faithful servant has long
en lame; and I have toiled beyond my strength.
or the last two days, I have been exceedingly
licted. The latent complaint, under which I
ve long laboured, has, at length, discovered
elf. It is an abscess near the neck of the bladder,
iich has now broke, and occasions me much
akness, and frequent pain. But I feel a power

take me out of the world whensoever it shall be for his glory. Dr. Baines and Dr. Pool prescribe me jellies and strengthening food.

"Dec. 19. The abcess is now become an ulcer, and, for the last ten days, my weakness has increased. Yet I am blessed with a cloud of mercies. My dear husband evidences towards me the most tender affection and deepest concern. He has left nothing undone that could alleviate my affliction. He attends me night and day, and prays, (if it be the will of God,) that we may not be separated at this time. For myself, I enjoy the calmest composure, having neither a wish to live, nor a fear to die. I have not felt the least murmuring during this affliction; but, on the contrary, peace, resignation, and the Spirit of prayer for my husband and the church: and, in particular, for the Methodist connexion. I have mourned to see a too great conformity to the world among them, and too much of human wisdom in the ministry, mixed with the simplicity of the Gospel. And for myself, I see that all I have done needs washing in the atoning blood of Christ. My soul is humbled on account of it, and I offer up my Saviour's sacrifice as my only plea. The poverty of spirit I feel, flows from a conviction of my utter unworthiness, and from a spiritual view of the purity of God.

"Dec. 24. What Dr. Baines prescribed has been of use. I am slowly recovering. A kind letter from Mrs. Grey, and one from Mr. Entwisle, and one from Mr. B. Newton, came this morning. I wept much in reading them, because of their kindness and affection; and my heart is affected with the kindness which has flowed from every quarter. The Spirit of prayer rests upon me for the church of God. May it rest upon me while I live. May the Lord visit his vine; the vineyard of his right hand planting. My heart can say,
 'Take my body, spirit, soul,
  Only thou accept the whole.'

"Dec. 27, 1806. My journal has been c for a whole year, during which time, I hav called to make the greatest sacrifice. M husband died on the 19th of March, aged nine years. God was purifying and prepari by my last affliction, for this great event dear husband's affection for me was great, a provision he has made for me is ample. Bu he is gone...... The evidence he gave interest in Christ, the assurance he felt, a prospects he had of the heavenly inheritance, the powers of my pen. Mr. James D. Burtc notes of his expressions, which have this yea published in the Methodist Magazine.

"During this stroke, I have felt the fr human nature, and have not properly im the event. During his affliction, of five I did not sufficiently offer him up to the but was too much elated whenever there wer of his recovery, and too much depressed these hopes were taken away. Thus I wen ward and forward, instead of looking for c power to say, 'If this cup may not pass fro liberty near the chapel, I took a small one in Leeds, and, with my servant Esther, learned to live alone, having spent all my life with a family.

"During this year, the sermons of Mr. Henry Moore were very profitable to me, particularly the one he preached on Abraham offering up Isaac his son. He observed, that after the patriarch had made this sacrifice, he never offended God in any thing as formerly. Hence he urged the necessity of living in the spirit of sacrifice. This came with great power to me, and enabled me to make fresh efforts, daily and hourly, to offer up my husband, whenever sorrow would have spread a gloom on my mind.

"About this time, a letter of our late sister Crosby, written soon after her conversion, fell into my hands, and very much supported me in resignation to the will of God. It was written in the year 1768, and addressed to Miss ******. 'The thing you want,' says she, ' is, to be freed from the refined, but inordinate love of the creature. This will procure you rest; for the Lord alone can unite the heart of friends. Blessed be his holy name, I do find that sweet rest in him; for I enjoy nothing but what has first been offered up in sacrifice to him. Thus I sweetly enjoy repose, and whatever earthly favours the Lord is pleased to confer, to continue, or to resume, I alike offer the praise to him, who is my life, and my all.' These words had a very consoling effect on my mind, and gave me fresh strength daily to offer up my husband in the spirit of sacrifice to the Lord. I have need to do the same with regard to my religious friends. While living in the superintendant's house, they often called, having business; now I seldom see them: I believe they do not love me less; but twelves, containing about seventeen sermons in the besides six separate sermons on various subjects. Since his death, the Conference at Bristol agreed that they might be re-printed, and sold by the preachers, if Mr. Entwistle would undertake it on his own account. The committee in London have declined printing them! This has tried me exceedingly, as the spirit of prayer was given me daily that they should be published.

"All I could now do was to write to about thirty of the principal preachers; and I rejoice to add, that they did approve of the sermons being printed; and many of them thought that they would rise in estimation, and be regarded, at a future day, as a monument of the simplicity and unction that attended the first preaching of the Methodists.

"July 2, 1807. My journal has been neglected, on account of the efforts I have been using to get my husband's sermons re-printed. Lately, retracing all the scenes through which he passed, and the triumph of his death, all my sorrows seemed to return; but, thank God, they were not unaccompanied with joys; the wine and oil of the kingdom were poured into my soul. I am now striving to live by the hour; and neither to look backward nor forward with anxiety: and as, from the nature of my complaint, life cannot be long, I would devote it to the best of purposes. My class has increased to eighteen members; and it is a consolation that I have strength to meet them.

"Feb. 14. I have been engaged in publishing two letters on relative duties, but chiefly on the duties of a woman to her husband and her children; and I have sent them to different circuits to be given away. They are addressed, as a token of esteem and love, to Mrs. Reece, with whom we have travelled in the London circuit. Mr. Reece approved of the publication; and Mr. Sutcliffe revised them for the press. But all my earthly toils draw towards a close. My complaint has returned with greater violence than before.

"Feb. 17. This is a fast day. Dr. Baines and Mr. Dickinson do not allow me to go out; therefore, I endeavoured to improve the time at home. My mind was sweetly drawn out after God. I felt a great desire to live nearer to him than ever; and he gave me a spiritual view of my hinderances, which I lamented in his sight. The day previous to my relapse, I experienced a sweet power to give up myself wholly into his hand, either to live or to die. Since my husband's death, I have been free from every earthly attachment, which would prompt me to live.

"I came to York on the 8th of June, and bore the journey better than I expected. Here I have to record the tender kindness and love of Mr. Grey's family, whose long friendship, and sincere piety, are deeply impressed on my heart. I owe much also to Mr. Robert Spence, who showed me every mark of affection and esteem, both for the body and the soul. I was enabled once to dine with Mr. Joseph Agar, whose heart and house have ever been open to the people of God. Mr. Mather, son of the late Mr. Alexander Mather, who is

" Mr. and Mrs. Pawson, of Thorner, have seasonably come to visit me. Esther, my old servant, is also very attentive.

" During the last winter, while reading over my journal, I have extracted whatever was most material concerning Mrs. Downe, with other remarks on a circle of religious friends, now in glory, and given them to Miss Lucas.

" My natural disposition is social, which has been confirmed by habit; but now, I have learned to live retired. I felt lonely at the first: but the Lord can make every thing easy. My mind is composed and happy from day to day, when I see hardly any friends. Such is the power of grace, if we yield to its influence."

☞ These are the last words in the journal of this most valuable woman, who devoted life and fortune wholly to God, after she was called by his grace. Her complaint brought her so low, that she could not talk much; but in resignation, prayer, and submission, she breathed her chaste and happy soul into the hand of that God whom she had served with a single eye, and most simple and ingenuous piety. She died, June 2, 1808, and was interred with her husband, at Thorner. I shall close this Memoir with the following account, drawn up by my friend Mr. Entwistle, who knew her well, and highly esteemed her.

" By humility, meekness, gentleness, Christian simplicity, deadness to the world, habitual spirituality of mind, and entire devotedness to God, she rose above the common standard of Christian experience and practice; and her latter end corresponded with her general spirit and conduct. Before the death of her beloved husband, she was much afflicted; and afterwards had several severe attacks of the complaint which terminated in her dissolution. In October, 1808, I paid her a visit; she was then recovering from a severe illness. The only thing she wished to see before she left the world, was a new edition of her husband's sermons; and when that was promised to her, she seemed to have every desire gratified. After spending several days with her, I took my leave, with inexpressible emotion, expecting to see her face no more, which so happened. Mr. Stanley, who visited her almost daily in her last illness, transmitted to me the following account:—' About three in the afternoon, June 2, 1809, died Mrs. P.' For some time she had been on the decline, and the nature of the disorder was such, as led her friends to expect that her death would be sudden. Of this Mrs. P. was also informed, and made it the subject of her conversation: not with terror and alarm, which those in bondage, through fear of death, would have done, but always with composure of mind, while every feature of her countenance beamed forth pleasure. Contrary to expectation, her death was gradual, which afforded me an opportunity of visiting her frequently, and of knowing the state of her mind, from day to day. During the whole of her illness, her faith was unshaken, her hope bloomed with immortality, and her consolations abounded. She evidenced, in her last moments, the most anxious solicitude for the prosperity of Zion, in her fervent prayers for it. The day on which she died I spent some time with her; she was perfectly recollected; her old friend, Miss L. was sitting by her. The first subject of her conversation was, her late husband's sermons, which were in the press; she was much pleased at it, and fully persuaded that the sermons would advance the glory of God. She prayed that the Lord would attend them with his blessing. She expressed her fears, that many of our people were falling into conformity with the world. At three o'clock in the afternoon her class was to meet in her parlour, to renew their tickets. I thought it improper for them to meet in the house, as she was dying, and proposed to meet them at another place; when, to our surprise, she said, "No! do favour me with this one thing, let all my class come into my chamber, and I will take my ticket also. I have been above thirty years a Methodist, and I shall die one." It was about ten o'clock when she said this: but while the members of her class were assembling, filled with sorrow, all expecting that this would be the last meeting they should have with her on this side eternity, she breathed her last, viz. about seven minutes before three o'clock. I proposed many questions to her, such as the occasion suggested, and received the most satisfactory answers. She said, 'My joy is not so rapturous as that of some I have known, and read of; but, I have no doubt, no fear, I am going to my blessed Jesus.' While we were at prayer, much of the divine presence was felt. Her soul was wholly stayed upon God: indeed, her end was such as every good man would wish for." I regret that I had not the opportunity of witnessing her divine comforts. Two years I lived in the house with her: in her, I saw how a Christian *lives;* and it would have been at once agreeable and profitable to have seen the Christian die. May my last end be like her's! Amen.

FINIS.

London: Printed at the Conference-Office, 14, City-Road, By Thomas Cordeux, Agent.